EX LIBRIS

Randy Manning

A Path Through the
Japanese Garden

Bryan
Albright
and
Constance
Tindale

First published in 2000 by
The Crowood Press Ltd
Ramsbury, Marlborough
Wiltshire SN8 2HR

This impression 2001
© Bryan Albright and Constance Tindale 2000

British Library Cataloguing in Publication Data
A catalogue record for this publication is available from the
British Library.

ISBN1 86126 316 3

Photo credits: all photos by Bryan Albright, except:
Noel Marten 17, 28, 58, 61 bottom right;
John Carter 11, 27 top, 44 left, 48, 59, 89;
Connie Tindale 111

All drawings by Bryan Albright

Edited and designed by
Focus Publishing
The Courtyard
26 London Road
Sevenoaks, Kent
TN13 1AP

Printed and bound by Times Offset, Malaysia

Contents

Preface

As I was preparing to write this book, I looked back to see if I could identify the time when I first became interested in gardens. As a child I lived in a top-floor flat in an old Victorian house in south London. If the landlady was in a good mood – and usually she wasn't – I was allowed to play in the rambling old back garden. Maybe that's why I now have such a great need to live in the country and work with natural things.

I became interested in the arts in my early teens and ever since have been particularly fascinated by Oriental art. When I was supposed to be in a painting class at my art school in London, I was usually to be found in galleries or museums. I spent my time searching either for those beautiful Chinese ceramics of the Sung Dynasty, or Japanese craft products, swords, kimonos and Ukiyo-e prints. Somehow, fine art lost its attraction and I felt more at home with arts that had practical applications.

In the early 1970s, I moved to the west coast of Canada, and spent a lot of time in the mountains, and on the small islands where the landscape is so similar to that of Japan. I was a city boy suddenly thrust into a dynamic relationship with an unforgiving natural world, but I felt surprisingly at home so close to nature. It woke something very deep inside me and gave me a different perspective on my life.

After returning to England in the late seventies, I became interested in Bonsai and to this day maintain a collection and study with a Japanese teacher. The rules and aesthetics of Bonsai are very close to those of Japanese gardens and it was this connection that first brought me to work on the construction of a Japanese garden.

One landscaper I knew was asked to build a garden for a Japanese school in Suffolk. Knowing that I was familiar with the types of plants needed, the pruning techniques and the design concepts involved, this designer asked me to work on the project. That was eighteen years ago. I went on to design and build many Japanese garden projects for private clients, and have created gardens for events such the Ideal Home Exhibition and the Motor Show. In 1995, the Japanese garden I designed and built for the Hampton Court Flower Show was awarded a Gold Medal by the Royal Horticultural Society.

Over the years I have written many articles on Bonsai and Japanese garden techniques for various magazines and have travelled to Japan to study and photograph them. This accumulation of material prompted my co-writer Connie Tindale to suggest that we collaborate on writing this book. Without her persuasive efforts, I probably would not have done it.

Bryan Albright

I spent my early childhood in the idyll of the cherry orchards of post-war Kent and had a plot of my own in a half-acre rose-strewn overgrown paradise. Then I was abruptly uprooted and thrust into the wastelands of the industrial north. Migration to London in the swinging sixties intervened, and it was many years before I regained the love of nature that I had had as a young girl.

I became involved in horticulture professionally when I went to work for Lord Walsingham at Merton Hall Gardens in the early 1970s. There, I was placed under the charge of Head Gardener Frank Grimwood. He was steeped in tradition, insisted on everything being done the right way and taught me more about plants and their needs than I can ever thank him for. Marriage, children and a career are not generally conducive to obsessive gardening but somehow I managed to combine them all, although not always successfully.

I left horticulture behind for full-time education and a subsequent post as Senior Lecturer in Business Studies at City College in Norwich. As my own garden developed and needed only maintenance rather than creativity, I became interested in the art of Bonsai. It was through my love of this art, and a need to develop my skills, that I met Bryan.

I have travelled extensively and, in addition to writing business-related instruction manuals, have written travel articles for magazines. Being a teacher, I wanted to pass on some of the knowledge that I had gathered from Frank Grimwood, and from my subsequent experiences, and I'm delighted that Bryan allowed himself to be persuaded to write this book with me.

Constance Tindale

Introduction

What is a Japanese-style garden? What does it look like? What emotions does it stir within you? Why have Japanese-style gardens fascinated Europeans for centuries and why has there recently been an enormous surge of interest in them? What is it in this ancient garden form that speaks to us so strongly on the verge of a new millennium? There are so many questions to be answered.

Most people have a mental picture of what a Japanese garden contains. Scenes are conjured with arrangements of rocks and pebbles, a pine or a red maple tree, bamboo, a lantern, and perhaps a deer scarer. All of these things could be in a Japanese garden but they do not in themselves make the garden Japanese in style.

What does a Japanese garden feel like? Most would say it is a quiet place; a timeless place with the sound of running water and a sense of order. Perhaps there is a clue here to what makes this style of garden so appealing. The Japanese garden is rooted in a time when rocks, plants and water were all considered as living things. In an ecologically conscious world, is this an ideal to which we are longing to return?

Did you have a garden when you were a child, no matter where or how small? Was it in a city among the cool dark shadows of towering buildings or in the country, with fruit trees and flowers intermingling in a riot of summer colour? Think back to those beloved plants that everyone used to have, but that you have not seen for so long. What were they called? Maybe you planted your first seeds in that garden and watched them grow and you knew where all the insects and birds lived. Perhaps you played there and enacted great sagas in the forest of plants. In your imagination, rocks became mountains and whole new worlds were created in a few handfuls of soil. I bet you remember quite clearly what that garden felt like.

Japanese gardens are like that. They are about experience: about feeling the way rocks and plants meld together, and about understanding their real relationship. Just as you instinctively find the place in a room where you are comfortable – where you like to sit – you will learn to trust your instincts about where a rock should be placed in the garden.

Would travelling to Japan to look at gardens, or even looking at beautiful pictures of the gardens, allow you to comprehend the essence of what is the Japanese garden? Perhaps a better way to understand the spirit of a Japanese-style garden is to make one, to live with it and to care for it.

Gardens are practical places where work is done but where we can, when we choose, experience exceptional peace and tranquillity. In the Japanese garden we learn about the natural world in a very profound way. This practical book aims to provide sufficient historic perspective and practical guidance for you to create a Japanese-style garden of your own. It is not the aim of this book to give a chronological history of the Japanese garden. However, a certain amount of history is necessary to understand the gardens' underlying design forms, simply because they are the structures upon which the garden must be built. Without a strong design the garden you create will become a pastiche of Japanese-looking elements, and a frivolous and dissatisfying thing.

In Japan, a strange amalgamation of styles reaches back over thousands of years; it helps to know about the influences that have combined to produce the widely differing examples of gardens. Some of those influences can be traced directly back to Neolithic times in an almost unbroken form. This is one of the reasons why Japanese gardens are so interesting. The Japanese garden can tell a story: a story so ancient that the beginning can only be guessed at. While our lives are changing so rapidly, and our whole environment is threatened, we can find solace in the constancy of something that has such a strong link to the past. The Japanese garden suggests a time when human beings were closer to the natural world.

It is right, at the very beginning of a practical book, to sow the seeds of what is at the very essence of the Japanese garden: its continuity. Continuity calls for maintenance, that continuously evolving process that happens after the garden has been built. A garden is constantly renewed by its maintenance; it is never finished, never complete, ever developing, never dying.

One image that comes to mind when considering this continuity is the ancient symbol of a snake or dragon swallowing its own tail.

CHAPTER 1

The Influences that Formed the Japanese Garden

THE LANDSCAPE OF JAPAN

Deep within all of us is a feeling for the landscape of our birthplace, and an instinctive attraction to specific types of landscape that trigger even deeper memories and emotions. For example, a city dweller who one year goes on a walking holiday in the mountains, and feels at home there, even though it is an alien environment, will appreciate the strength of this inner feeling.

Japan has a very broken coastline. It is fundamentally a long chain of large islands, each with tiny offshore islands of their own. These islands sit on a chain of volcanoes, aptly named the 'ring of fire', which surrounds the Pacific. A broken spine of mountains called the Japan Alps runs through the centre. Mountains and islands set in a sea are part of a pattern used in garden design that is rooted in the Japanese landscape, and inseparable from it.

The country also has a wide climatic band that creates varied environments. In the north it is almost tundra, while in the south and in Okinawa it is almost subtropical, with snow-topped mountains and hot, dry plains. Volcanic activity leaves the islands subject to violent meteorological disturbances such as tsunami and taifun tidal waves; (the word 'typhoon' is derived from the latter).

This unsettled environment has led to the development in Japan of a certain type of architecture, in which natural products such as wood, paper, bamboo and reeds predominate. The inventiveness with which these products have been used is truly amazing. A strong element of Japanese culture is concerned with taking a few simple things and combining them in infinitely different and innovative ways. It is almost like manoeuvring the characters in a play. These natural materials were

Opposite: The Japan Alps – the Snow Country.

used virtually exclusively until the Meiji era (1868-1904), when all things Western became popular. Most Japanese people still desire to have at least one room of their home in a traditional style, if they can afford it, and these natural materials are still used today in temples and in traditional-style houses.

Set against this architecture is the garden. It is often the juxtaposition of the straight lines and geometric shapes of the architecture against the natural forms of the plantings that gives the Japanese garden its particular tension of design.

PREHISTORY AND SHINTO

In ancient times, man had a more intimate relationship with the natural world. Shinto, Japan's indigenous religion, has its roots in those times. Shinto was not just a religion, but a way of life. It had neither scriptures nor founders, but kami or 'sacred power'. Kami is an honorific for noble and sacred spirits who are adored for their virtues and authority. People honoured the mountain because it was the source of the water that irrigated their fields, and they honoured the sun because it brought light to the darkness and its heat made the crops grow. They honoured their ancestors because ancestors had gained knowledge that could be passed to their children of how to survive in their unpredictable world. Anyone and anything that was 'outside of the ordinary' could become kami.

In the Orient, there has always been a willingness to venerate nature's extraordinary places or unusual formations. Rocks with strange shapes, or trees with abnormal growth, were seen as most likely places for the kami to live. As a consequence, these objects were often sectioned off from the surrounding area by ropes or rows of small stones, which defined the area as a sacred place. These sacred places, using the

Left: *Pond garden at Kyomizu Temple in Kyoto.*

Opposite: *A Chinese garden. Sun Yat Sen garden, Vancouver, Canada.*

beauty of the shrine's surroundings, took the mind from the mundanity of everyday living to a higher divine plane.

Tales were handed down from the ancestors about their journey to colonize Japan's island groups. They probably gave rise to various concepts of the 'sacred islands', which, together with the veneration of 'sacred ponds' of life giving water, is thought to have formed the pattern for what became the first gardens. Underlying forms even from Neolithic times (5000-4000BC) can still be found in gardens that are being constructed today in Japan

CHINESE INFLUENCES – BUDDHISM AND MYTHS

There are written records of gardens in Japan dating from the first century AD, but the oldest of the gardens still in existence is from the Nara period of the eighth century. With the introduction of Taoism to Japan, and the spread of Buddhism from China, the stage was set for the first temple gardens. Myths had great influence on, and provided a popular focal point for the design of many gardens.

The ancient Taoist myth of the 'Islands of the Blest' is especially significant to garden design. According to this ancient myth there were, somewhere far off the eastern coast of China, five islands that at one time floated free on the great ocean. Mariners who chanced to come close to the islands saw them only dimly, as they seemed to be enveloped in strange luminous mists. The main island had at its centre three great mountains; here could be found the springs of life giving water, and the fungus li chi, the eating of which bestowed immortality. It was said that the islands were inhabited by men and women who, having attained immortality, lived together in total harmony. Their bodies were pure white, perhaps even transparent; they were as light in weight as thistledown and flew about on the backs of cranes. All the animals that lived in these islands were also pure white.

For various reasons, the ordering power of the universe caused the islands to stop floating free; they become fixed to the backs of giant sea turtles, which constantly carried them around. These turtles were replaced by other sea turtles every sixty thousand years. The ordering powers subsequently caught the turtles in a net and allowed three of the islands to drift away while keeping two islands close by.

'Islands of the Blest' in a private garden.

Unsuccessful expeditions to find the islands were mounted by several Chinese Emperors. An early Taoist writer Lieh Tze wrote that he believed he had found them east of the gulf of Chilli, beyond the eastern horizon. According to him, they were set in a mythical sea into which flowed all the streams of the world, including the great celestial river of the Milky Way.

Although in the original myth these 'Islands of the Blest' or 'the Immortals' numbered five, when this theme was taken for later Japanese gardens they became represented by just one or two islands. The two islands were symbolized by the crane and the turtle, representing two seemingly opposite forms of energy. The crane is spontaneity, eccentricity and dynamic action, while the turtle is stability, endurance and longevity. Observation of the animals in question brings understanding of the action and reaction of these cosmic energies.

When one island was depicted it usually represented 'the mountain at the centre of the universe', Mount Meru from Hindu cosmology, or

Opposite: *Horaizan – the mountain at the centre of the universe. Zuiho-In Zen garden, Kyoto.*

Zen dragon. Painted wall screen, Ryogen-In Temple, Kyoto.

Horaizan, from Buddhism cosmology. The mountain at the centre of the universe is found in creation myths from all the tribes of mankind and is perhaps the most ancient creation symbol accessible to us. It is the solid land arising from sea – the formed arising from the formless, or the unconscious becoming conscious.

With the arrival in Japan of the Buddhist Amida sect, what is known as the Pure Land form of Buddhism began to develop. The Pure Land was Amida Buddha's place of rebirth. It was seen as a paradise of magnificent palaces set in beautiful gardens with shady terraces and lotus-filled ponds. It was not considered as ethereal but as tangible, and visions of this paradise became the inspiration for many gardens. The recently restored and reconstructed garden of Heijo-kyo was originally built in about 750BC and is typical of the type of building and pond combination of that era. Another preserved building and pond complex from the same era is the temple of Byodo-in, south of Kyoto.

By the beginning of the Heian era (AD 794–1185), several influences were in place for the design of gardens. Among the inspirations were the landscape, the islands in a sea, the sacred islands and ponds from ancient times, and the Taoist myths of the 'Islands of the Blest'. In addition, there was the mountain at the centre of the world, as well as paradise visions of the Pure Land, or the mandala from Buddhist cosmology. The mandala is a circular drawing representing all the worlds and levels of consciousness, often represented by concentric rings.

All of these symbols are reflections of archetypal universal forces, as are all the elements of ancient myths. In reading or in listening to a myth, there is empathy with these elemental forces; a similar elemental empathy is experienced in the building and the contemplation of the Japanese garden, in the 'experience' of the Japanese garden. (Later chapters show how these forms manifest themselves in the first garden type, the Shinden pond garden.)

Zen stone garden. Ryogen-In, Kyoto.

ZEN

The rise of Zen Buddhism during the Kamakura period (AD1185–1336) had a significant influence not only on the Japanese garden but also on the whole of Japanese culture. Zen became increasingly more important as the influence of the Pure Land sect began to wane. Zen was brought to Japan from China (where it is known as Ch'an Buddhism) by the monks Eisai and Dogen in the early thirteenth century.

The teachings of Zen are about stripping away all that is 'unnecessary' in our life, and achieving the Buddhist goal of seeing the world in a state of consciousness where thoughts move without leaving a trace. Gone is decoration for its own sake. What is left is the essential nature of things – 'just as it is', without embellishment. Basically, Zen is a mixture of Buddhism and Taoism.

China, during this period, was in the middle of the Sung Dynasty and enjoying a great flowering of the arts. The Chinese ink-wash paintings of the Sung Dynasty, where vast mountain landscapes were represented with just a few brush-strokes, were to be a major influence on gardens in Japan. Garden makers sought to create gardens that were like the painting's minimally represented landscapes. Because the gardens had become smaller and covered little space, the landscapes became miniaturized, but that does not mean they just became model-like replicas. The landscape had to be suggested by other means: mountains were represented by rocks, and the sea was implied by the use of wave shapes raked in gravel. A whole landscape could be represented by a few carefully placed items.

The dry stone gardens created under the influence of Zen are probably what most people in the West think of as Japanese gardens. The form of these stone gardens is called Karesansui, which translates as 'withered mountain water'.

Although in some cases actual reconstruction of natural features can be found in gardens of this period, it is this idea of things being 'represented' that is one of the keys to understanding the Japanese garden.

Raku tea bowl, made by Konyu Raku (1857–1932).

Opposite: Tea garden. Designed by Bryan Albright, Hampton Court Flower Show, 1995.

TEA

The last major influence on the development of the Japanese garden is the Tea Ceremony. Tea drinking is believed to have been introduced into Japan from China around AD700 by Buddhist monks. Tea played a significant part in Buddhist mythology – the first tea bushes were thought to have sprouted from the eyelids of the Buddhist patriarch Bodhidharma, who had cut off his eyelids in mortification at having fallen asleep during a period of meditation. Monks, using tea as part of rituals that venerated the founders of Buddhism in India, may also have used it as a mild stimulant to help themselves keep awake during long meditations.

Later, tea drinking was put to use in lavish entertainments and as part of a secular ceremony that was loosely based on the early Buddhist rituals. It was not until about AD1400 that what is now called Cha-no-yu, or the 'Way of Tea', was developed. These ceremonies were first held inside the large houses but later, small specially designed houses were built. The first purpose-built tearoom was set up in 1489 in the Silver Pavilion villa in Ginkaku-ji Garden in Kyoto.

Over the past five hundred years, the Tea Ceremony has undergone many changes. In the beginning, famous tea masters such as Rikyu, Oribe and Enshu developed elaborate rituals for the presentation of tea. Rikyu replaced precious Chinese tea utensils with homely craft ware like peasant rice bowls from Korea. He made his tearooms considerably smaller, and brought the preparation of the tea into an intimate circle of guests. His guiding aesthetic was wabi, one of those Japanese words that is difficult to define, but may be suggested by the words 'impoverished charm' or 'honest ordinariness'. Or perhaps the following Haiku poem represents it:

> *a gust of wind*
> *the white dew on the autumn grass*
> *scatters like a broken necklace*
> **(Bunya no Asayasu AD 900)**

The tea masters also developed various styles of garden in which to situate their teahouses. These incorporated innovative features, to ensure that the passage from the entrance gate into the teahouse put the participants in the right frame of mind for the ceremony. Many of the features of these tea gardens became used in other types of gardens.

CHAPTER 2

The Main Garden Styles

Internal and external influences on Japan all contributed, therefore, to the creating of the Japanese garden. The main styles of garden that developed from those influences are often categorized, but in reality the divisions are blurred as is inevitable in anything that is constantly growing and changing. The Japanese garden is certainly metamorphic. In the Edo period (1615–1868) and the Meiji period (1868–1904), these divisions became even more blurred, with garden styles from earlier times being copied and combined. The various garden forms from all ages can now be found in contemporary gardens. The garden designer works with the form. The design is the language of that form. The techniques used are simply the vocabulary of the language. A garden form can be used at any time and in any place as an entity in its own right because a garden form is never fixed.

This section is devoted to a selection of gardens that specifically typify each of the styles. It is not meant to be a comprehensive guide to the gardens of Japan – they are far too extensive. It is simply meant to demonstrate something of the feel of the main styles by using the most famous of the gardens as examples, and should help with your own designs.

SHINDEN – POND AND ISLAND GARDENS

The name Shinden comes from the architectural style of the villas of the nobles of the Heian period (AD 794–1185). Few gardens have been left from this period, but one fine example is Byodo-in, on the Uji River, south of Kyoto. This temple complex and garden, originally built in 1053, gives some idea of the paradise gardens of the period. Unlike the palaces of that time, which faced south according to the Chinese rules of Feng Shui, Byodo-in, being a

Opposite: *Shinden-style temple at Joruri-ji.*

temple, has its main buildings orientated to face west.

The palaces were light airy places that looked out on bright south-facing courtyards, and then across a pond that usually had one or more islands, often connected by bridges. These ponds were used for boating parties, and the surrounding gardens were designed to be seen either from the boats or when strolling around the ponds. The gardens had a very natural feel and were designed to integrated comfortably into the surrounding landscape. The ponds themselves were excavated so that water usually flowed into them from the east and out of them to the south-west, again in accord with the code of Feng Shui.

The simple elegance of the period is shown in Joruri-ji, another temple garden from the Heian era, built in AD1107. The main hall, which contains nine statues of the Amitadha Buddha, overlooks a pond edged with water-lilies and styled pine trees. In the pond is a small island with a simple stone group.

Kinkaku-ji, 'The Golden Pavilion'.

The 'Dragon's Gate' waterfall, and the 'Carp Stone'. Kinkaku-Ji, Kyoto.

Opposite: *The main rock group, Daisen-in garden, Kyoto.*

Pine-covered islands, Kinkaku-Ji.

Across the pond is situated a wooden pagoda, and the whole complex nestles comfortably into the surrounding Cryptomeria forest.

By AD1400, much more extensive pond gardens were being built. The group of buildings and ponds at Kinkaku-ji, or the 'Golden Pavilion', started life as a nobleman's villa but was later converted into a Zen temple. The main pond is dotted with small islands, on which are grown beautifully styled Japanese red pine trees; the islands are topped by rock groupings constructed to resemble the turtle and crane islands from the myth of the 'Islands of the Blest'. Other notable features of this site are the famous 'Dragon's Gate' waterfall, with the 'Carp Stone' at its base, and the teahouse.

In Chinese mythology, the carp (or trout) climbing the waterfall back to its spawning ground became symbolic of the struggle against adversity in life. Passing through the threshold of the 'Dragon's Gate' was also symbolic; it represented an initiate passing into a special society, or a student gaining entrance into a seat of knowledge such as a university.

KARESANSUI – DRY GARDENS

Towards the end of the Muromachi period (AD 1333–1573), a style of garden evolved that is now referred to as Karesansui. This type of arrangement, with extensive use of rocks and gravel, had existed from much earlier times but only as a small part of other gardens. The form came into its own, and became the style that in the eyes of Westerners most often typifies the Japanese garden. The sparseness of the designs owes much to Sung Dynasty ink-wash paintings and derives from the minimal concepts of Zen. Most of these gardens were, therefore, originally built in Zen temples.

Boat-shaped stone.

Opposite: *Rock group at Daisen-in.*

Many of these gardens were designed for viewing either from a limited or fixed vantage point, often within a building or from a narrow veranda. Planting was kept to a minimum, using mosses, a few clipped bushes and sometimes a styled pine.

An important garden in this style is Daisen-In in Kyoto, which was probably completed around AD1500. The garden stretches around the abbot's quarters and is incredibly narrow, only three metres deep. The garden unfolds like a scroll and

movement around the garden is as if on a journey, taking in each sight as it comes. The garden is said to represent the 'River of Life', which flows from Horaizan, the mountain at the centre of the universe. The river tumbles from the mountain over a dry waterfall and under a bridge, and then splits and flows past a 'crane' island. The flow of the river broadens after the first rush of youth, flows past two turtle islands and then passes under what is now a covered wooden bridge, to part of the abbot's

quarters. This feature is a reconstruction, which was added later in an attempt to re-create how the garden looked in earlier times. As the river emerges, a curious stone in the shape of a boat is seen sailing past another stone grouping that represents the 'Islands of the Blest' myth.

The most famous of the dry stone gardens is Ryōan-ji, 'The Temple of the Peaceful Dragon'. It is a later form that was developed from the garden at Daisen-in. It has a collection of fifteen rather small rocks in a flat 'sea' of white gravel. The only plant in this garden is the moss that surrounds some of the stones. This garden seems more enigmatic perhaps than any other of the dry stone gardens. It seems almost to go beyond a representation of myths or an actual landscape, and to have been built solely to evoke a meditative state. The ultimate in minimalism is the Tokai-an garden, which is just a blank expanse of gravel where the mind constructs its own garden.

SHAKKEI – BORROWED SCENERY

Another interesting concept in Japanese garden design began to emerge in the Muromachi era – 'borrowing' scenery from the surrounding landscape. This idea, Shakkei, or 'borrowed scenery', was later developed into a fine art form in the Edo period. The original descriptive word for the garden form was ikedori, which literally translates as 'to capture alive'. Distant scenery is 'captured' by a specially designed device, which is an integral part of the garden, and is thereby incorporated into the overall scheme. The scenery is then no longer just a view from the garden but appears to be a part of it, enlarging and enhancing the whole. Reaction to the captured scenery will differ from person to person, as each will have an inner response to what they are seeing.

The captured landscape feature could be a distant mountain, hill, plain, seascape or even a temple building. Whatever scenery is selected for incorporation into the garden must be clearly defined in the basic design so that the best method of capture can be used. There are various methods of capturing different types of scenery; the concepts behind them are described further in Chapter 3.

Opposite: *Ryoan-ji Zen garden, Kyoto.*

ROJI – TEA GARDENS

The drinking of tea and the creation of the Tea Ceremony brought about a garden form that was not only innovative in its own right, but also influenced other later styles such as the courtyard garden, and the hermitage-style garden, a rustic form of the stroll garden. The term Roji means 'dewy path', and the sole purpose of this garden is to act as a pathway to transport the participants of the Tea Ceremony from the outside world into the inner world of the ceremony. Everything in this garden is geared to bringing about certain calming psychological effects within the viewer.

The garden is divided into two parts – an outer and an inner Roji, which are separated by some kind of fence and gateway. Entry to the outer Roji is through a main gate, which is then shut when the last participant has passed through. Each of the two parts of the garden has a different character. The outer area is usually more open and light and the inner is more enclosed and secluded, reflecting a deeper movement into the centred state of mind required for the ceremony. Passing first down a slightly formal path to a waiting bench, participants wait for the ceremony to begin. When everything is ready, they are led through the middle gateway, the chumon, to the inner Roji, where the teahouse is situated. In this inner area are located a freshwater well or spring, and the tsukubai. The tsukubai, which literally means 'to make double' or 'bend over', is the place where participants bend to wash in ritual purification. It is an arrangement of a water basin, the chozubachi, and a group of stones, or yakuishi.

The passage through the garden is often via stepping-stones, which are very skilfully placed precisely to control the speed and direction of walking. These inner gardens are sometimes damp mossy places with ferns and luscious green planting. Flowers are rarely seen in this area, as they would detract from the poignant display of ikebana, or flower arrangement, usually found in the tokonoma, the display alcove in the teahouse. Sometimes, these gardens are simply stones and pounded clay with no planting at all, as in the Hananoe Tea Garden.

Everything must be clean and in its place before the ceremony, so that there are no distractions for

Tsukubai in Hananoe Tea Garden, Hagi.

Nitobe Tea garden, Vancouver, Canada.

the participants of the ritual. Fallen leaves and dust have been swept away into the chiriana or dust pit, which is effectively more symbolic than functional.

Lanterns in tea gardens are made of stone, or occasionally of wood or bronze. These lanterns were originally found in Buddhist temples, but later became incorporated into the gardens. They are used for guiding passage along the paths, and to illuminate the water-basin feature or tsukubai.

The overall feel of these gardens is usually simple and rustic, echoing the style of the teahouse architecture. Later, the architectural style of Sukiya took its feel from these simple teahouses and gardens. Teahouses are widespread throughout Japan and are often to be found in part of a much larger garden. Large gardens were built in this style, incorporating this feeling in order to achieve refined rustic elegance. The most famous is the Omoto Senke School of Tea in Kyoto.

For an explanation of how to construct a tsukubai and a description of the types of water basins, see Chapter 5.

KAIYUSHIKI – STROLL GARDENS

To achieve maximum effect, the gardens of the Heian period were meant to be seen from a vantage point such as a boat on a pond. To achieve the same effect, the Karesansui gardens and Shakkei gardens had very limited viewing points, often restricted to one only. Unlike either of these, stroll gardens, in the Kaiyushiki style, were designed to be viewed as an unfolding series of tableaux. The idea of a 'walkaround' garden may have originated in the Heian period, but as time passed it developed into a complete form of its own.

Reflecting the Japanese fascination for miniaturization, these gardens often included small-scale reconstructions of Japan's or China's beauty spots. Frequently, the garden's series of features would be linked by a theme; in Edo times, the gardens became very popular as miniaturized re-creations of Buddhist pilgrimage routes. Views, or set-piece compositions, were revealed with progression around the garden; after being revealed, each view was then hidden, and a new scene was unveiled with each turn. Merit was acquired in walking this miniature pilgramage route, just as it would have been in walking the real thing.

By the time of the Edo period, these gardens had become grand affairs that were often built around a lake with islands. Here, the views to be seen might

Stroll garden at Kenroku-en in Kanazawa.

have been reconstructions of famous sights such as Mount Fuji or Ama-no-Hashidate, or 'The Bridge to Heaven', a spit of pine-covered land off the coast of Japan. Cherry or Ume groves, groups of rocks representing Chinese myths, or Shakkei views of surrounding scenery would also have been featured.

The pathways around these gardens also became very inventive, with bridges and stepping-stones across streams, with stone lanterns and water basins beside them. Later gardens in this style became symphonies of variations on themes, leading to dramatic climaxes.

There are many existing examples of the stroll garden, including Kenroku-en in Kanazawa. The reason for this is that during the Meiji era many large gardens were turned into public parks in imitation of parks in Western cities. For ways of incorporating some of these ideas into your own garden, see Chapter 3.

TSUBONIWA –
COURTYARD GARDENS

In some ways, the concept of the defined space of Neolithic times echoes through what would become the Tsuboniwa or courtyard garden. The courtyard garden is a feature that can be found even in Heian times. Courtyards enclosed by the outer wings or structures of the Shinden palaces often contained just one plant or species of plant. For example, the Hagi Tsubo was a courtyard with Japanese bush clover, the Yomogi Tsubo, a courtyard with Artemisia, and the Sasa Tsubo contained only Kumasasa bamboo. These courtyards were usually bright places, open to the south, and sprinkled with white gravel. Court ladies who occupied the rooms facing these courtyards were sometimes named after the flowers that grew there.

Later, small areas of garden were created alongside Zen temples. These small courtyards became arrangements of plants, rocks, gravel and paving usually symbolizing Buddhist cosmology.

During the Edo period, the courtyards of houses developed into secular forms of the Tsuboniwa. There was a need to bring light and air into the rooms that surrounded the small courtyards. Plants brought a change of air into the courtyards, and, with the introduction of decorative water features, the invigorating power of running water enlivened these closed spaces. Small tearooms off the house became

Small Zen courtyard garden. Daisen-In, Kyoto.

popular with the increasing fashion for a tea ceremony that was now secular.

Three main elements were borrowed from the tea gardens for these small gardens: the lantern, the water basin and the stepping-stones. In the tea gardens these were all functional components, but in the Tsuboniwa they became decorative elements, to be used in abstract compositions. The lantern brought light and a feeling of well-being, and the water enlivened and refreshed the area. In the rainy season, the stepping-stones kept feet out of the mud in these damp confined areas.

In contrast to the small gardens used for the Tea Ceremony, the Tsuboniwa was a garden intended to be viewed from the house. It was conceived from the elements of the tea garden, but its function was completely reversed. Everything in the tea garden was aimed at controlling the participant towards the tea ceremony; looking out on a garden would only have been a distraction.

Courtyard gardens can still be found in the old areas of Kyoto behind some shops and restaurants, and in the courtyards of many temples. The idea has also been used by many modern Japanese garden designers for spaces in new restaurants and offices.

Courtyard garden at Four Seasons nursery, Kent.

CHAPTER 3

Designing the Garden

How will you find the design for your Japanese-style garden? Where do you begin? It may seem strange, but the design will usually find you. All the various elements that have been chosen will come together and, somewhere along the way, a design will mysteriously appear. If you ask all the right questions, the garden will be a sum of all the answers. It is necessary to make a big leap of faith when working this way, but the resulting garden will be very satisfying. This is truly an adventure, and its outcome is not known at the beginning. The finished garden will fulfil what is required of it from all standpoints: from you, the site and the materials used.

BASIC DESIGN QUESTIONS

Improvization, and taking advantage of chance happenings and thoughts, is quite acceptable in the East, where random happenings are treasured as acts of 'God' that fit in with varying philosophies. In the West, there is a greater emphasis on forcing things to conform to some 'grand design' that has been thought out beforehand. It is rare that one person can truly pre-visualize every eventuality within a garden, so 'go with the flow', and do not be afraid to change your basic plan at the last minute.

Several questions need to be asked before beginning your design:

- What type of garden do you already have?
- Are you going to be able to integrate a Japanese-style feature?
- What type of feature do you want to build?
- What can you actually achieve?
- Will you build the garden yourself?

THE DESIGN

Look at the site you are going to use. If it is small and enclosed, or can be sectioned off by walls or fences,

your task is easier and you can use almost any design style that you wish. The obvious style to use for a small space in the city would be the courtyard garden, using surrounding walls as a plain backdrop, showing off the features you choose. In a confined space, it would be wise to use only two or three main elements in your composition, keeping the design strong. Stick to one main concept. Having too many things going on in a small space is distracting.

Think about the style of the garden. Japanese design can be broken down into three classifications: shin, gyo and so, or, respectively, formal, semi-formal and informal or rustic. Tea gardens, for example, are generally gyo, or semi-formal, or so, rustic in nature.

For a larger area, first ask yourself what you want from the garden. Do you want a pond garden, a dry garden, or will the garden have a theme like the 'Islands of the Blest'? Do you want a landscape or a completely abstract composition? Is the garden to be viewed mainly from one place or will it be like a stroll garden, with many little features and vistas with seating areas? Could the concept of Shakkei, or 'borrowed landscape', be used? Having considered these questions, you can now start to look at the actual garden you want to build.

The basic design of the garden has to be strong and well conceived, because everything else will hang on this. Start by measuring the site's area and drawing a plan. This will help you to get in 'touch' with the site and its possibilities, and enable you to assess its 'feel'.

Landscape

You will have to consider, and decide upon, the type of landscape you wish to depict in your garden. Will it have a horizontal or a vertical feel? The horizontal landscape is very quiet and restful on the eye; the vertical has strong shapes that reach upwards, and has a more powerful dramatic effect.

If your budget is limited, a few attractive and

Shin, or formal style.

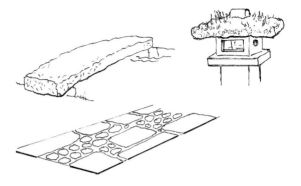

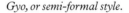

Gyo, or semi-formal style.

So, or rustic style.

A simple horizontal landscape based on a rocky coastline.

carefully placed small rocks can be set in a horizontal design to good effect. The idea is to create a grand landscape in a small space, without spending grand sums of money. However, you must have a strong vision to make it work. Consider your design ideas, and study any available photographs of Japanese gardens to see if your ideas are feasible.

Many Japanese gardens are deliberately planned to be seen from only one viewing point. With this in mind, the framing of the landscape scene is of vital importance. Several devices can be used for framing purposes – for example, the window frames or balcony supports of the house from which the garden is to be viewed could be utilized

A vertical landscape, based on high mountains.

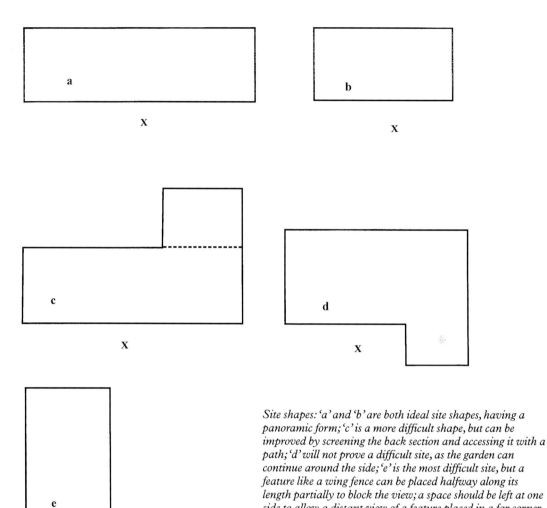

Site shapes: 'a' and 'b' are both ideal site shapes, having a panoramic form; 'c' is a more difficult shape, but can be improved by screening the back section and accessing it with a path; 'd' will not prove a difficult site, as the garden can continue around the side; 'e' is the most difficult site, but a feature like a wing fence can be placed halfway along its length partially to block the view; a space should be left at one side to allow a distant view of a feature placed in a far corner. X is the main viewing side.

in this way. Unwanted or offending features on the sides of the site can be screened off by fences.

Site Shapes

If, like the Daisen-in garden, your site is scroll-shaped – wide but not deep – it is ideal for a landscape garden as it already has the panoramic shape you require. If, however, the shape of your site is less than ideal, there are usually ways around the problem. With a square site you can fool the eye into believing that the site is wider than it actually is. The simplest way of achieving this is to reduce the site's depth by running a fence or similar screening device such as plantings

across its middle. The back part of the site could then be used for other purposes. Another way to disguise the shape would be to obscure the far corners of the area with soft planting, keeping the front area as wide and uncluttered as possible.

Tricks with perspective can be employed to gain the effect that you want and to fool the eye into believing that it is looking at a great landscape. When looking at landscapes, objects that are close by appear larger, while things further away appear smaller. Placing larger items at the front of the garden area and smaller items at the back will create an illusion of depth. If you are designing for a narrow passage area you can reverse this effect by putting larger things in

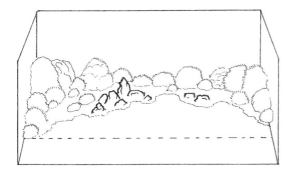

Obscuring the far corners.

Improving a deep site by dividing with a fence.

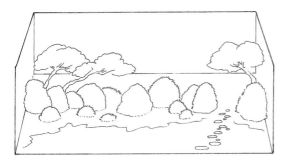

Improving a deep site with a planting barrier.

Making a pond appear larger by obscuring one side.

the distance, thus shortening the space considerably.

Objects near to the observer appear more detailed and precise, while things further away appear more blurred and simple in shape. This is due to atmospheric conditions, but the phenomenon can be copied in your design. A painter will tell you that warm colours tend to appear closer than cold ones. This may have its roots in the subconscious – to do with memories of distant blue mountains – and can also be used in your design.

The eye is also tricked when items are overlapped. Overlapping suggests depth, for example, when overlapping mountains recede into the distance. This device is often used to make a pond appear larger than it actually is.

By blocking the view of its sides the pond appears to be a great lake because the eye believes it probably

Various screening devices for obscuring edges.

stretches far beyond its actual limits. Forcing the eye to travel a greater distance is another trick for making the space seem greater than it actually is.

Strong Points – The 'Golden Section' and Asymmetric Triangles

The next step is to work out where the garden's strong points are. This can be done by dividing the area (see below), and will give some idea of where the main features, such as rock groups, should be placed. Any one of the strong points can be used for the location of the main feature.

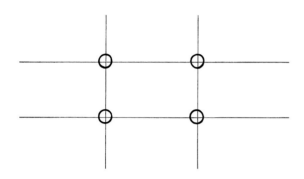

Strong points found using (above) thirds, and (below) the 'Golden Section'.

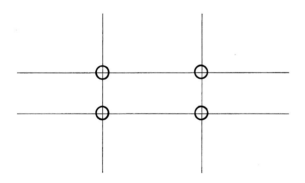

In the illustration above, the point in the garden where the main feature, such as the rock group, should be placed is found by dividing the area into thirds. One of the main points can then be chosen as the location for the feature.

In the second illustration above, the strong points are found using the 'Golden Section'. It can be seen that, from a design point of view, this adds more tension to the proportions. Almost all Japanese design is asymmetrical, based on the scalene triangle or the 'Golden Section'. A rough guide is to place things in proportions of 2:3 or 1:3. This throws the emphasis of the garden over to one side and leaves a balancing empty space on the other. This deliberate asymmetry, which was also used to great effect in the paintings of the Sung Dynasty, creates a dynamic movement in the design while retaining a visual balance. The design also looks 'natural'.

For instructions on how to calculate the 'Golden Section', see the boxed text opposite.

Emphasizing the Oriental preference for the use of uneven numbers creates a sense of potentiality. Symmetry and even numbers give a sense of rigidity and of the hand of man.

Nature is always changing and moving forwards, and this is what the Japanese garden is trying to suggest, while at the same time achieving, through balance, the feeling of order and timeless tranquillity – a natural flow. For design purposes, most aspects of the Japanese garden can be broken down into triangles. The more asymmetric the triangle, the more dynamic the movement. (See below.)

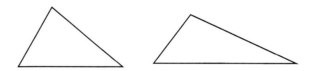

Asymmetric triangles.

Shifting the weight of emphasis to one side allows the opposing open spaces to 'speak' and bring dynamic movement to the design. A natural object

Direction of flow of objects.

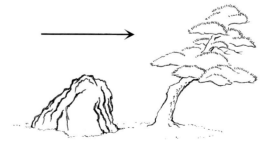

'GOLDEN SECTION'

To find the 'Golden Section' proportions of a garden, draw a line AB (see Fig 1 below), which represents the length or width of the site. Draw another line BC at a ninety-degree right-angle to line AB (see Fig 2 below). BC should be exactly half the length of AB. Complete the triangle by drawing a line AC.

Set a compass for a radius equal to the line BC and draw an arc from point C through the line AC. The line AC will have been bisected at point X (see Fig 3 below).

Reset the compass so that it will now give a radius equal to AX and draw an arc from point A to bisect the line AB at point Y (see Fig 4 below).

The line AB, which represents the proposed garden, now has the 'Golden Section' marked at Point Y.

This measurement is useful for deciding on the placement of many items in the garden, and will give tension and strength to the design. It can be used not only in appraising the overall proportions of the garden but also, for instance, in finding the relative heights of rock, lantern and water basin arrangements.

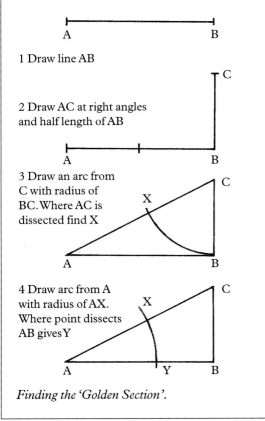

1 Draw line AB

2 Draw AC at right angles and half length of AB

3 Draw an arc from C with radius of BC. Where AC is dissected find X

4 Draw arc from A with radius of AX. Where point dissects AB gives Y

Finding the 'Golden Section'.

always has a direction of flow. Flow is fundamental to a Japanese garden and its principles must be strictly adhered to when planning and placing objects. If stones are to be placed in a group, they must conform to a direction of flow within the group. Also, the group of stones as a whole must be correctly positioned at one of the strong points in the garden.

Try to make sure that all the main lines of flow in the design are outwards, as this will allow the landscape to expand. If you block a flow, the landscape will shrink and the mind will not be able to roam freely.

You can now start to look at all the elements in the garden in terms of their mass and direction of movement, and how they interact with one another. Choose something you like as a starting point. Your favourite rock may suggest a theme, a story or an abstract vision of distant mountains.

Often, rhythms in the architecture of the house can be echoed in shapes in the garden; a feeling of unity between the house and the garden should always be sought. The garden should not be divorced from the house and often there can be a very positive integration of the house and garden, with one starting to flow into the other. If the garden is totally enclosed in a courtyard this is not such a problem, but integration into the whole should always be considered.

Shakkei or 'Borrowed Scenery'

Shakkei is another technique to consider when it comes to building a design. It is rarely used, except in large gardens, but it is worth looking at even if just for the inventiveness of its concepts. There are six major ways of using Shakkei or captured scenery, as follows.

Tree Trunks
A distant view, such as that of a mountain, can be incorporated into the garden by using a frame to show off a carefully selected portion of the landscape. One device involves planting trees effectively between the garden and the desired view. This may seem to defeat the purpose by obscuring the view, but, as the trees grow, the mountain will be seen through their trunks. This has the effect of placing a deliberate positive visual device between the garden and the view, 'capturing' it.

A good example of this technique can be seen in the garden of Entsu-ji, where the distant scenery is brought into the garden design by the use of middle-ground tree trunks.

Captured scenery using tree trunks.

The Sky

The sky can also be used to capture a distant mountain. In the ink-wash paintings of the Sung Dynasty, the empty spaces give a poignancy and heightened meaning to the object shown. When capturing with the sky the same feeling is needed and the proportion of sky to landscape is critical in making this work. The visible areas of sky and landscape must not be equal; if they are, they visually counteract each other. If the mountain is close, proportions of six parts landscape to four parts sky could be used, and would work well if the view of the mountain was off-set. If a more distant lighter effect is required, the proportions would be reversed, using up to seven parts sky to three parts landscape. If the mountain is in the middle of the view, rather than to the left or the right, this device cannot be employed as it would divide the area into two counteracting parts. In this case, trees should be used to capture the scenery.

Capturing distant scenery by using a man-made object.

An Object

An object such as a Japanese lantern can be used to capture landscape; placed in the middle distance, it will draw the eye from the garden into the landscape to be captured. The effect of the 'capture' can be reinforced by relating the object used to a similar object in the garden, for example, another lantern. This technique is used to good effect in the garden of Joju-in, which is part of the Kiyomizu-dera complex of temples in Kyoto.

Rhythms

It is possible to capture the view of distant landscape by echoing its rhythms in the placement of rocks or other features in the garden. However, the strength of

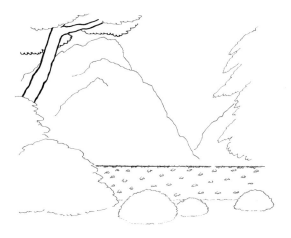

Capturing distant scenery using the sky.

the rhythms and counter-rhythms must be well defined and positively felt.

Architectural Features

Parts of buildings, such as eves or the posts that support a veranda roof, can be used to capture scenery

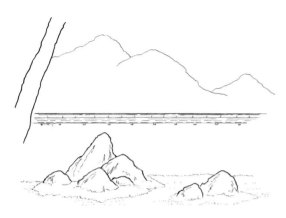

Capturing distant scenery by echoing its rhythms in the garden features.

if the main viewing point of the garden is at the house. A good example of the use of this feature is the capture of Mt Hiei in the garden of Shoden-ji in Kyoto.

Middle-Ground Objects

Features outside the garden, such as small copses or groups of trees, can also be used to link a view and the

Capturing a distant view using architectural features; here, the wall and the building frame the distant mountain, bringing it into the garden design.

garden. However, this can be a difficult device to use, as it usually cannot be sufficiently controlled by the gardener. Trees on neighbouring properties, for example, have a habit of growing too large and obscuring the view to be captured, or may be cut down.

Computer Packages

A number of garden-design computer packages are available on the market. However, there is a temptation to forget that the computer is only a tool. The packages are good for quantifying how many slabs will be needed for a path or how many bags of gravel and sand might need to be bought. They work well when dealing with large numbers of similar items, but are far less effective when dealing with items that need to be carefully and aesthetically placed. The better packages will allow the movement of items within the design so that some idea of spacing can be gained with a three-dimensional perspective on the results. However, rocks of different size and plants with contorted shapes can only be accurately placed when they are actually on the site, as they need to be related specifically both to the site and to each other.

Packages with comprehensive plant illustrations and listings are particularly useful for finding the right plant for the right spot, but the site of a Japanese garden must be 'felt' and its 'character' recognized before a design can be finalized. No computer package can do this.

Capturing distant scenery using middle-ground features, such as a copse of trees, to attract the eye.

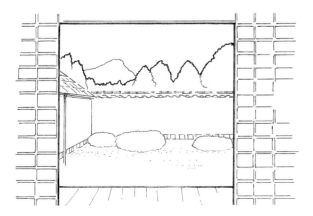

CHAPTER 4

The Main Elements of the Garden

STONES

When planning and designing your garden, the stones must be the first items to be placed. Plants change shape and texture over the years, fences and artefacts are periodically replaced, but the stones are enduring and usually remain where they were first placed. The rocks in the diagram below all relate to the main rock and to each other, contributing to an asymmetrical balance.

Choosing and Placing Stones

There are some dos and don'ts for placing stones. Use stones of different sizes, stones that have the same characteristics, and stones that have similar features. This usually means acquiring stones from the same location. Mixing different types of stone can produce interesting results but it is very difficult to get a coherent final look. To relate two stones to each other successfully is relatively easy. To relate three stones is more difficult. To relate five stones is an art, and, if they are of different colours and textures, takes great skill. Do not be over-ambitious; the simple idea usually works best and speaks loudest.

Use stones with character. The best stones are ones that have been naturally weathered by wind or water. Unfortunately, there is no tradition in the West of valuing stones for their aged appearance, and many

Left: *The direction of visual movement of rocks within a group.*

Setting out the main rocks.

potentially good stones are moved by bulldozers or tipped off lorries. The Japanese prefer dark, hard stone and their garden stones are highly prized and handled with great care. On the rare occasions that they do change hands, large sums of money are involved.

Freshly quarried stone usually looks too harsh but in Japan there is such a demand that it is possible to get stones that have been artificially 'weathered'. This is done by placing quarried stones and sand and water in what looks like a giant tumble dryer and rolling them for many days. The results are quite convincing.

The placing of stones is a great art but can be intuitive. Learn to allow yourself to feel the relationships of the rocks and follow these simple rules:

● Always place the main stone first. All other stones then relate to this.

● Do not place stones in straight lines and do not use even-sized spaces between them, as this destroys the illusion of space.

● Try to place the stones in triangular formations. A single rock might not have much movement in its shape but if it is placed together with another this can create a movement (see illustration on opposite page).

● Examine each stone to find its best side and to establish its top and bottom. A stone placed on its 'head' will always look unstable and feel wrong.

● If you are using a vertical stone, it will need a foundation of other rocks to balance it (see illustration on page 41).

● Always bury the bottom of the stone in the ground. Stones sitting on the surface do not look stable and certainly do not give the impression of being part of the landscape. Understanding the way stones should be placed is fundamental to a Japanese garden. The concept is far removed from the piles of rock that often pass for 'rockeries' in Western gardens. Prime examples of misplaced rocks can be found in some of the hideous excuses for landscaping that are found outside many shopping centres and motorway service areas.

● Stones of similar character should be placed together. Rugged stones represent young dramatic mountains, while rounded stones suggest an older more stable landscape.

● Bear in mind the size of your garden and choose stones that are in keeping with its dimensions.

Your design must always tell a believable story. Do your rocks really look like mountains? Remember, most of Japanese garden design is based on landscape, however abstract this may become in the final garden.

Stones are commonly placed in groups of 2, 3, 5, 7, and so on. One of the most favoured stone groups is made up of three stones and is called sanzon. It originally represented the Buddhist trinity. Large numbers of stones are often subdivided into smaller groups of 3, 2, 5 or 3, 7, 5, and so on.

In the ancient texts on Japanese gardens, the shapes of all the stones used were given names. These names referred to the stones' specific functions in the design, or to their shapes. They 'said' something to the gardeners of the time, and the names were interwoven in both Japanese culture and religion; we can now only guess at their roots.

In a re-creation of the 'Islands of the Blest' myth in

Two typical three-stone groups.

A five-stone group.

garden form, the islands can take their underlying shape from the animals of the myth. The characteristic of the Turtle Island is a rounded, stable shape with a definite direction – the direction of the turtle's head. The turtle's 'legs' tend to further stabilize the shape and to integrate it with the surrounding rocks. The Crane Island, in contrast, is a more dramatic arrangement and usually has more upright stones. Although the underlying shape is said to be that of an animal, this is only an analogy to explain the actual shape or movement of the whole stone group.

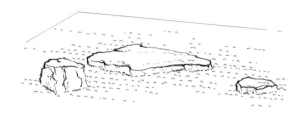

A low stone group.

Turtle-shaped island.

Crane-shaped island.

A tall stone group representing the 'Islands of the Blest'.

Yin yang stones, symbolizing the balance of forces in the universe, are also common, as are stones representing astrological features such as Ursa Major (the 'Plough'), or Buddhist cosmology symbols. Some rocks are placed so that they coincide with astrological features at certain times of the year.

Everything in the garden can be just the thing it is or it can speak from a more ancient level of myth and storytelling. It is up to you to choose the approach with which you are most comfortable. The Japanese garden is not just a design exercise because it can express so many ideas.

Setting Stones

When setting stones, the main stone should be set first and the other stones should be related to it. If the stone has sufficient below-ground bulk of its own to support

An island with a strong vertical stone that is used as the main focus of the garden usually symbolizes the mountain at the centre of the universe, Horaizan. Single stones of special shape can be placed in the garden to represent objects, such as treasure ships (as seen in the Daisen-in garden), or fish, as in the 'Carp Stone' of the Kinkaku-ji garden. A stone in the Joju-in garden in Kyoto represents the shape of an eboshi, a type of headwear from Heian times.

Beautiful rocks and a pine trained in the shape of a boat. Kinkaku-Ji Temple, Kyoto.

Visually stabilizing tall stones with smaller side stones – the rock on the right has become visually more stable by the addition of smaller stones at its base.

it at the desired angle, packed earth may be enough to keep it in place. If not, the stone can be set into a concrete pad to lower its centre of gravity. As the stone is being set, move around it and check its alignment from all angles. Lifting gear will be needed to place large stones, and the preparation of the site will need to have been completed, and concrete laid, before the stones are finally positioned. If you are working on made-up ground, or ground that has been severely disturbed, do not forget that this will settle and compact over time. Compensation for this settling and compaction will have to be made when you originally set the stones.

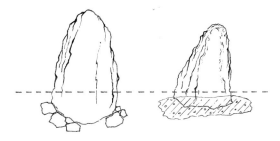

Setting stones using small rocks or concrete.

Setting large stones.

Wide formal paths. The Philosophers Walk, Kyoto.

PATHS

Path Styles

Paths are always important, but the paths of the Japanese garden demand particular care and inventiveness, as they are a passageway through the garden's unfolding beauty. The number of different variations on path design found in the gardens of Japan is awesome. Oriental playfulness over rearranging a few simple shapes in an infinite number of combinations manifests itself strongly in this area of design.

Paths can be grouped into formal, semi-formal and informal types; pathways near the house should generally be more formal than paths that are further away. If the garden is designed to be quite flowing, geometrical paths are the most suitable as they act as a good contrast. However, if the garden is very rustic in nature, the paths may simply be made of randomly placed natural stepping-stones similar to those found in tea gardens. Consider the type of garden you want before deciding on the type of path that you use.

A path is often the design element that gives movement to a flat area. If a path runs straight to its destination, it will appear to be too abrupt and rude. So, if a long path has to lead directly to a building, it is better to be as indirect as possible and approach the building at an acute angle.

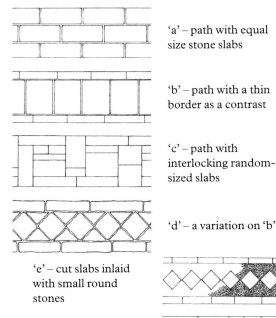

'a' – path with equal size stone slabs

'b' – path with a thin border as a contrast

'c' – path with interlocking random-sized slabs

'd' – a variation on 'b'

'e' – cut slabs inlaid with small round stones

'f' – random yet controlled pattern with diagonals

'g' – a small stone border

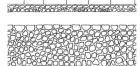

'h' – similarly sized small stones making a visually exciting path

Examples of formal shin-style path designs: 'a' – path with equal size stone slabs; 'b' – path with a thin border as a contrast; 'c' – path with interlocking random-sized slabs; 'd' – a variation on 'b', with hand-cut slabs; 'e' – cut slabs inlaid with small round stones; 'f' – random yet controlled pattern with diagonals; 'g' – a small stone border; 'h' – similarly sized small stones making a visually exciting path.

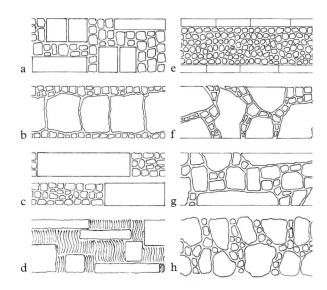

Some semi-formal gyo-style path designs: 'a' – a contrast of crisp-cut stones against rough-cut smaller stones in a regular pattern; 'b' – large flat stones allow a smooth walking surface; 'c' – a contrast of long straight slabs and patches of smaller stones; 'd' – a path with roof tiles on edge in a random pattern; 'e' – a visually exciting path controlled by formal side stones; 'f' – large slabs contrasting with small inner stones; 'g' – long edge slabs helping define the edges of a path; 'h' – a more rustic version of 'b'.

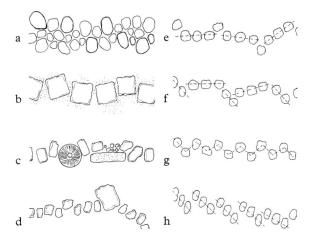

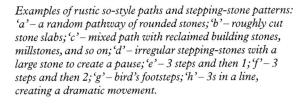

Examples of rustic so-style paths and stepping-stone patterns: 'a' – a random pathway of rounded stones; 'b' – roughly cut stone slabs; 'c' – mixed path with reclaimed building stones, millstones, and so on; 'd' – irregular stepping-stones with a large stone to create a pause; 'e' – 3 steps and then 1; 'f' – 3 steps and then 2; 'g' – bird's footsteps; 'h' – 3s in a line, creating a dramatic movement.

Careful placement of the stones that make up the path can control the speed of walking through the garden. It can also be used as a device to direct the eye, dictating the direction from which a person views the garden's scenery. This particular use of pathways is brought to a fine art in the stroll garden, where different scenes are revealed, then hidden, as others are unveiled, as the path winds its way around the site.

Building a Path

When setting stones in the path, try to avoid junctions where the corners of four stones meet. The strong visual emphasis created by the four corners meeting disturbs the visual flow of the path. Above all, the path must feel right for the feet. Passage along a path is sometimes broken by a larger stone, referred to as the 'path-dividing stone', which acts as a junction for another path or marks a place to pause and view a particular feature in the garden.

Formal or semi-formal paths, and any other paths that will get a lot of foot traffic, must be set out properly to avoid subsidence, cracking and subsequent injury to people using them. First, the ground must be prepared by removing any turf or plant matter and the finished height of the path must be determined. It will help if some wooden stakes are set, and a string line is used to map out the shape and dimensions of the path. This line should be set at the correct finished height of the path. The path's eventual height can be calculated as being the depth of the thickest stone used, plus 25mm for the mortar on which the stones have been set, 50mm for the concrete base and 75mm for the hardcore below that.

Drainage can be a problem, and rainwater will gather on the path if no provision for drainage is made. Any surface water will freeze in the winter and will be dangerous, as well as possibly causing damage to the path. To overcome this problem, the path can be cambered slightly from the centre – a drop of 13mm over 1m should be sufficient. Care must be taken that the camber is not lost when pointing of the stones takes place.

Rustic path in a tea garden. Nitobe, Vancouver.

Path detail.

Paving detail. Representing a bridge between house and garden.

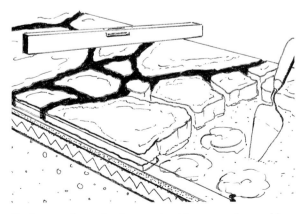

Setting a path over hardcore and a thin concrete base – this path is laid on a concrete base and the stones are pointed with a coloured mortar mix.

If soil needs to be dug out and removed so that the path can be laid, this must be done next. The hardcore is then laid and rammed down with the head of a sledgehammer or similar heavy weight. Concrete can then be laid and levelled on top, to a depth of 50mm. A good mix for the concrete would be 5 parts combined aggregate (sand and ballast) to 1 part cement.

Setting Paths

The stones can be laid once the concrete has hardened. If they are in a formal pattern then this needs to be marked out and the stones placed to make sure they fit the design. At least 15mm must be left between each of the stones for the pointing. Larger stones should be set by placing blobs of mortar mix on the concrete. Place four roughly at the corners and one in the middle of where the stone is to be set. Smaller stones might only need one large blob to seat them. A mix for the mortar would be 5 parts sharp sand to 1 part cement. Position the stone and

Old stone path. Hananoe tea garden, Hagi.

gently tamp it down with a mallet, checking that it is correctly aligned both with the string line and with the other stones. Checks should also be made to make sure that any 'fall' built into the design for drainage is retained.

After the stones have set firm, usually overnight, the pointing can be carried out. A mortar mix is made up of 3 parts soft sand to 1 part cement, with a little plasticizer added if necessary. The mortar should be recessed to about 10mm below the surface level of the stone to make sure it stands out visually. This recessing also helps drain away surface water. Try to keep the surface of the stones free from cement and use clean water to wipe away any mistakes before they dry. This will avoid the path looking messy.

Cement colouring can be added to the mortar mix to complement the colours of the stones used. The liquid colours are stronger and easier to blend than the powder ones are.

Stepping-Stones

Stepping-stones are usually used in informal settings, to suggest a footpath in the country or through the mountains. Although stepping-stones can be set in a variety of patterns, straight lines should be avoided as this imposes a formal pattern on to an informal design.

If the stones are thick enough, they can be set straight into the earth, although this would require a minimum thickness of 150mm. Once the stones have been laid, the earth should be rammed around them until they cannot move. If the stones are being set into a lawn, they must be set at a height that is clear of the blades of the lawnmower.

If the stones are not sufficiently thick, a pad of concrete will need to be placed in the earth as a foundation. When the concrete is set, the stone can be placed on it using mortar to bed the stone at the correct height. If the ground is already firm, this concrete pad needs to only be about 50mm deep and to be 50mm bigger all around than the stone. Place a few blobs of mortar on the concrete and tap the stone into position. Always check for level. Stepping-stones set within a gravel path also look very good. Again, these will need to be set, and boards should be inserted to retain the gravel.

When you are setting stones, take note of the spacing between them. Remember that not everyone has the same length of stride. Correctly placed stones make walking easy, while incorrectly spaced stones make the walker uncomfortable and detract from his or her enjoyment of the garden. Subtle changes in the spacing can act psychologically to change the mood while walking, from haste to reflection. The Japanese pay great attention to the variations in spacing, in order to hasten or slow passage through different areas of the garden.

Gravel Paths

Gravel paths can be an inexpensive alternative to stone slabs; again, proper preparation needs to be made if they are to be successful. The path will need at least 40mm of gravel with 75mm of hardcore beneath it. Excess soil should be removed. Wooden edging boards can retain the gravel; these should be dark in colour and of 150 x 20mm timber treated with wood preserver. They will usually be set about 10mm higher than the finished height of the path, but no higher than that. Wooden stakes 25 x 25 x 250mm long should be hammered in behind the boards to hold them in place, and then fixed with galvanized nails. Place the stakes 500mm apart. Pack down the hardcore and then spread and roll the gravel.

Bark Chippings

For woodland walks, bark chippings of 10-30mm can be laid to a depth of 75mm. Again, wooden edging boards may be needed to retain the chips and the ground below the chippings should be compacted.

FENCES

Fence Styles

Generally, the function of a fence is to delineate the division between two different areas or spaces. The type of fence needed is determined according to the use of those areas. For example, a fence may be essential to separate livestock from predatory wild animals; to maximize its effectiveness, the fence would need to be high, very strong or covered with

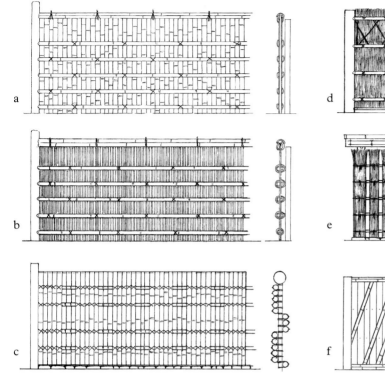

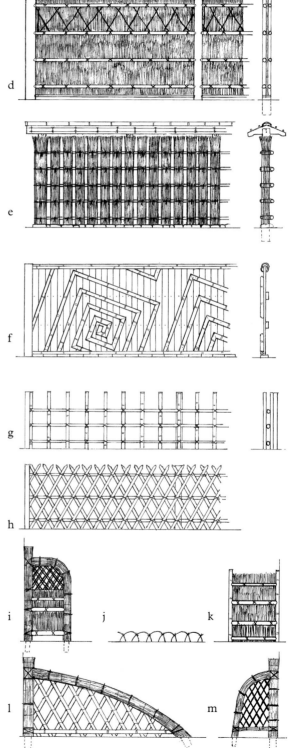

Above: *Formal-style fences: 'a' – Kenninji fence (named after Kenninji Temple); 'b' – Shimizu fence (named after a thin type of bamboo); 'c' – Teppo (rifle barrels) fence.*

Above right: *Fences Semi-formal style: 'd' – Takeho (bamboo branch) fence; 'e' – Taimatsu (torch) fence; 'f' – a modern design, made with split bamboo pinned to a board fence.*

Right: *Rustic-style and sleeve fences: 'g' – Yotsume fence (four eyes); 'h' – Yarai (stockade) fence; 'i' – Sode (wing) fence; 'j' – Nakano fence (named after an old weaving style); 'k' – Sode (wing) fence; 'l' – Koetsu fence (named after a famous craftsman of the sixteenth century); 'm' – small Sode (wing) fence.*

sharp protuberances. Its construction would be different if its function was to show the division between two neighbouring properties, to act as a windbreak, or to screen a particular view.

Without doubt, the inventiveness that the Japanese have brought to the making of fences is unsurpassed, and it can now be considered as an art form. Many of these fences have their roots in traditional functional designs, but have now become truly decorative. In the

hands of the Japanese garden maker, a few elements put together in an infinite number of permutations becomes almost a form of play. Fences can be used for many purposes – to enhance the natural forms of plants by contrasting them with the geometric forms of the fence, for example, or to evoke feelings of the countryside by suggesting rustic farm buildings.

Today, over one hundred designs of fence are known or used, many of them dating from as far back as Heian times. Perhaps the greatest amount of inventiveness has been in the design of fences for the tea garden, where subtle patterns and textures have been used to enhance the overall mood of the garden.

Building Fences

Traditional-looking fences can be home-made although the cost of materials is quite prohibitive. Usually, the material used for fencing is bamboo, but this can be combined with tree branches, wooden poles, planks, woody shrubs or reeds to produce a wonderful array of textures. Bamboo grows like a weed in the East, but the costs of importation to Europe put its price above that of wood. In addition, many bamboo importers are not very adventurous when it comes to stocking unusual varieties and other products such as bamboo branches.

Think about growing your own bamboo. It will grow in most climates, but it will be four or five years before you have a crop, and a single plant will not go far if you plan to make a fence. A number of the clump-style bamboos such as Arundiaria murielae will produce a substitute for the thin canes used in some fences; its branches can also be used instead of the bamboo branches found in various rustic-type fences.

The other alternative is to buy sections of ready-made fence. The sodegaki (wing fences) are easiest to come by, arriving in a convenient unit form. Japanese-made fences are very expensive even in Japan, but cheaper, less professional, alternatives are available from Malaysia and Thailand. These are still expensive compared with larch lap panels. Bamboo fences will not last for ever, but if they are well made and well cared for they may endure for ten to fifteen years.

Opposite: *Simple wing fence. Nitobe tea garden.*

Another way to tackle the problem is to invent your own style, or to adapt local products such as twigs, and the products of coppicing such as chestnut or willow, into Japanese styles. Local thatching reeds, such as Norfolk reed, can also work well as substitutes for Japanese materials. Fencing wood such as larch, which is available as de-barked poles, split poles and thinly cut planks, can also be used. Roofing-tile battens, available from builders' merchants, ready treated with preservative, are handy for making various type of latticework trellis. This approach is quite acceptable and is in the Japanese tradition. The aim is to build the garden in a Japanese style, not simply to create a collection of Japanese artefacts.

Before designing and constructing fences, it is wise to consult local building regulations. Generally, fences should not be more than 2m high, or more than 1m if they adjoin a public thoroughfare. Fences can, of course, also be used as windbreaks if the site requires it. Remember that the optimum benefit from a windbreak fence is felt at a distance about eight to ten times the height of the fence.

Oiling is a recommended way of preserving the bamboo fence. If the fence is washed down with water containing a fungicide, or weak bleach solution, before oiling, this will kill the moulds that could discolour the fence.

WALLS

In the Japanese garden, walls not only provide a more substantial barrier than a fence, they also provide a good plain background against which features can be shown. Traditionally, Japanese walls were made of clay and topped with a thatched roof or tiles. The beautiful warm earthy colour of the dried clay provided a harmonious background for use with the greens of plants, and walls were often embedded with broken roof tiles to give a pleasing pattern.

Japanese temple walls were whitewashed and a white wall has become a standard background for many gardens. Contrasted with the silvery appearance of the aged cedar beams used in constructing the temples, the white wall can provide a strong background for more monumental features such as rock groupings. The white wall acts like the

New blockwork wall.

unpainted areas in the Chinese ink-wash paintings and, in a good composition, it says as much as the feature itself.

The busy visual texture of European brick walls tends not to be a good background for the Japanese-style garden. However, crumbling old brickwork bearing moss or small plants, and walls of old cobblestones, do convey a mood of the antiquity that is so valued in Japan. Stone walls, if they are old, give a good background as long as the texture of the stone suits the garden's other textures. This is especially true in a 'rustic' garden.

If a new wall has to be constructed for your Japanese garden, concrete blockwork with a rendering of sand and cement will provide a good, and relatively inexpensive substitute for the traditional wall. Concrete blocks can be purchased already coloured in earth tones, and these can also provide a good background.

If an old wall is in situ, but not really suitable as a background for the garden project, it can be faced and painted a suitable colour. Rendering with sand and cement is one option, but this can be relatively short-lived in some regions if it has not been properly applied, as frost will tend to break up the surface after a few years.

Opposite: *Old clay wall, Kyoto.*

Another, better alternative is to batten the wall and face it with concrete panels, which are then painted with exterior paint. The panels are made of concrete mixed with a strengthening fibre and are about 6mm thick. They are easily drilled and fixed with screws. To prevent water penetrating the under-battening, joints between the panels can be covered with strips of treated wood. This also gives an appearance closer to that of traditional temple walls.

To cap the wall, tiled roofs can be constructed using small trusses made from treated wood with tile battens placed over them. Japanese tiles are expensive to import but second-hand English and Belgium earthenware ones are available from suppliers of reclaimed building materials. The beautiful traditional roofs with their regional patterns and 'guardian spirit' ridge tiles are hard to duplicate, but many interesting old ridge tiles and fancy corners are still available from European reclamation companies. These can be used in inventive ways, in the spirit of the Japanese gardener.

For a more rustic look, another type of roof can be constructed using wooden shingles. Machine-cut cedar shingles are readily available but, occasionally, the more beautiful hand-split larch or cedar ones can be found. These will last a long time if they are properly fixed, as the wood used is resistant to weathering and fungal attack. In North America, hand-split wood shingles are easier to find, especially in the west and in Canada, where they are usually made from Redwood (*Sequoiadendron giganteum*), Western red cedar (*Thuja plicata*) or Douglas fir (*Pseudotsuga menziesii*).

Study photographs of walls in existing Japanese gardens before deciding which style fits your own design. Detailed instructions on how to set the foundations and build a wall can be found in any good do-it-yourself book; the technique required will differ, depending on the style of wall you choose.

GATES

Many types of gateway can be found in Japanese gardens, including ones of modern design, but, whatever type you use, it must be in harmony with the wall or fence that it penetrates. Usually, the most convenient gates are of wood and several different traditional types are now available ready made from Japan, Malaysia and Thailand.

Various styles can be constructed quite easily. A traditional chumon gateway can be made with two upright poles and a simple shaped crosspiece. Simple gates can also be made from cedar boards or latticework bamboo. Many gates have a small thatched roof over them that is traditionally made from cedar bark strips or reeds, often held in place with a bamboo framework.

ENTRANCES

The first thing to be seen when approaching a house is the entrance. Where land prices are high, as in Japan, gardens tend to be small, especially in city areas; of necessity, much has to be made of a small area. In such small areas, keeping the theme simple allows the visual impact to be very strong.

The entrance arrangements in a Japanese garden can follow the same concept as the Tsuboniwa courtyard garden (see page 28); these are very popular with restaurants and any houses that are set back from the road. The eye is drawn away from the house and into the garden by setting a feature such as a lantern in a strong visual position. The design is kept crisp, and evergreen plants are used; this means a minimum amount of garden maintenance, as pruning once or twice a year, with a general regular tidy-up of dropped leaves, is sufficient. Styled trees or clipped bushes are also used, but these tend to be ornamental varieties that are carefully maintained so

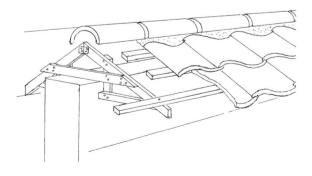

Tiled roof.

Opposite: *Concrete panel wall.*

Shingle roof.

Roof tile detail (Kyoto).

that they never out-grow their location.

This principle is put into practice in the front-garden areas of temples, restaurants and private houses. It usually takes the form of two or three main elements, such as a path and a type of plant, with a lantern or water basin. The path is usually of quite a formal appearance and often does not approach the

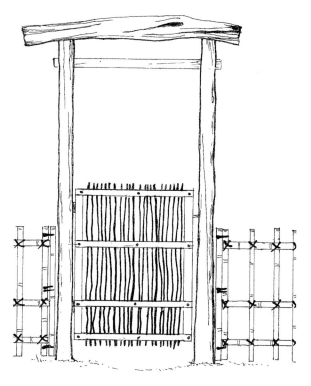

Chumon gate.

house directly but meets it at an angle, or changes direction midway. Evil spirits travel in straight lines so, without the bend in the path, they would rush along it and go straight into the house. Here, the influence of Feng Shui geomancy aids the design principle. A straight path with everything at ninety-degree angles to it is visually static. A carefully designed entrance shifts the emphasis from the front door to an appreciation of the garden/house combination. The mood will then be set for entering the intimate surroundings of the building, where worldly matters will be left outside.

At many of the Zen temples, the entrance route is

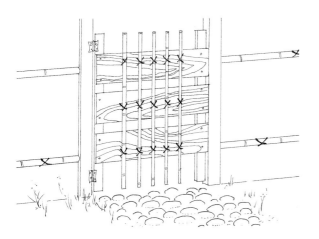

Cedar plank gate – a cedar plank gate with vertical bamboo poles.

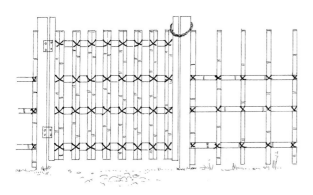

Bamboo lattice gate – a simple bamboo gate goes well with a yotsume fence.

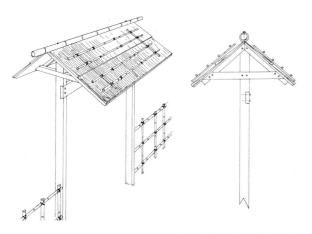

Gate with roof – a gateway roofed with ready-made reed panels.

The entrance to a private house, Kyoto.

quite long and convoluted so that the temple cannot be seen directly. The gateway often only presents a frame for a picture of the garden, which is in the form of an abstract arrangement of a styled tree with perhaps a beautiful rock, ground-cover planting and a pathway, all set against a plain wall. Following the path around a corner, the visitor is presented with another small picture, this time perhaps of a rock and a small fern. Around another corner is seen the entrance to the temple at the end of a long path. This circuitous route encourages the visitor to be in the right frame of mind before entering the temple itself.

GRAVEL

In dry landscape gardens, beds of sand or coarse gravel can be used to represent clouds or water, with raked ripple patterns representing the water's movement. It is often this blank plane of flat gravel that shows off various three-dimensional objects, such as rocks and clipped plants, to their best advantage.

Abstract patterns raked into the gravel can also be used to great effect, bringing interest to the quieter areas of some designs. Designing and raking these areas can be great fun, although it can also be mentally and physically very demanding. The pattern has to be held in the mind, and the correct sequence of strokes judged and applied with complete fluidity. Any hesitation in this duty is obvious and will show up in the final result. Very complex patterns require

Clipped trees.

Zen temple entrance.

Restaurant entrance.

A private house entrance.

Raked gravel – gravel can look very effective in small areas, but it must be meticulously laid.

Examples of raking patterns for gravel.

an almost meditative state – it is easy to understand why the discipline of raking temple gardens was part of a monk's training.

Choosing Gravel

It is possible to use sand for raked areas, but rainfall quickly destroys the patterns and a great deal of effort can be wasted. Coarse white sand is used to very dramatic effect in some gardens in Japan, including Ginkaku-ji, but this requires a lot of maintenance. It is better, therefore, to use coarse gravel. Many of the Karesansui gardens of the Zen temples use crushed granite of up to 20mm grain size. This is surprisingly coarse, but it is very effective, and readily available in Europe. Crushed granite is quite light in colour, but the small black specks of mica in it stop the gravel areas being too bright. Other stone types can be used apart from granite. Crushed slate graded to 20mm can look very good for a darker effect, which works even better when the surface is wet. Always check that the colour of the gravel works well with the type of rock that you are using.

Whatever type of gravel you decide to use, 6–8mm should be the minimum grain size; if the area is large, or you want a very coarse effect, 12–14mm should be the minimum to consider. Rough-edged chippings retain raked patterns better than rounded grains.

When ordering gravel, a weight of 15kg per 1cm depth per square metre coverage should be sufficient. However, it is always best to try a test area before ordering and then to allow some extra just in case the same gravel is not available again.

When gravel arrives from the stone merchant it is usually quite dirty and needs to be washed thoroughly before spreading. If you try to wash the gravel with a hose when it has already been spread, the dust particles may block up whatever drainage you are using, or remain in a layer under the gravel and provide a good place for weeds to take root. Slate is usually particularly dusty and needs washing well.

Laying Gravel

If you are planning to use gravel as a ground cover, or you plan to do a raked gravel design, you will first need to prepare the ground. Clear the area of any weeds, plants or turf. Make sure that the area is flat and reasonably level: a slight slope will help with drainage. Remember to allow for the depth of the gravel, as you will add 10cm to the height of the ground if you are doing a flat covering, and 15–20cm to the height of the ground if you are raking it into patterns.

Traditionally, the area to be covered with gravel was spread with clay and pounded into a hard surface. Today, three main alternative methods are used: a concrete base; Mypex, or a similar porous weed-suppressant membrane; or cement powder mixed into the surface soil. The third method is not really a very good idea in the long term, and it will be damaged if you decide to rake the gravel. If a concrete

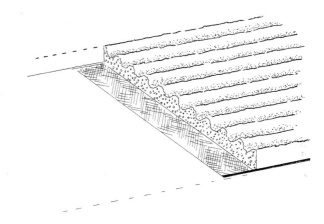

Laying gravel on a weed-suppressant membrane.

slab is laid under the gravel area it must be slightly sloping in order to drain away any rain that might gather on it and cause puddles to form. Some provision will probably also be needed to take the rainwater to a nearby drain.

The easiest to use of the available methods is the weed-suppressant membrane. If the area is large it must be prepared by laying 20mm shingle to a depth of 100mm. The membrane can then be laid on top of this. If the area is very large, flexible land

Setting out a large area.

drainpipe should also be laid in the shingle, and connected to a storm drain. The desired gravel can then be laid on the membrane. Lay enough gravel so that, if you are raking, the membrane will not be exposed.

Tools for Raking

Rakes required for raking gravel are of a special design, and not generally available in Europe, so you will have to think about making them yourself. This is not complex and the illustration below should help you to construct one that is inexpensive and serviceable.

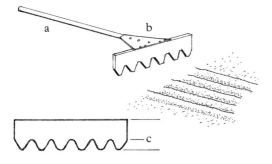

Home-made rake: 'a' – a stout broom handle braced with a piece of plywood and fixed with screws; 'b' – this depth needs to be at least 8cm. The rake head can be made from 18mm plywood, braced along the top edge with a strip of wood to take the screws from the handle bracing; 'c' – this depth needs to be the same as the depth of groove you require. Do not make the rake head too wide as the amount of force needed to pull the rake will too great.

BRIDGES

General Principles

In a Japanese garden, the bridge is more than just a way of getting from one side of a stream to the other. A bridge can be symbolic of crossing from the known to the unknown, or it can symbolize transcendence of the spirit to a higher level of awareness. In accordance with the great Taoist myth of the 'Islands of the Blest', the islands originally depicted in the Japanese garden were not joined by bridges. However, over the centuries, the islands became linked, perhaps suggesting that there were means by which man could attain immortality.

Japanese bridges, like fences, have become a source of great inventiveness of design and can be of formal shin, semi-formal gyo, or rustic so styles. The more formal styles are often copies of Chinese bridges. They can be made from wood or stone, have clean lines and may be decorated with quite rigid stylized designs. Some of these wooden bridges were painted red and this has, unfortunately, become a cliché of Japanese garden design in the West.

The rustic styles can also be made from stone but in this case the stone will be a roughly broken block that is reminiscent of one that might have conveniently fallen across a river in the mountains. Other rustic styles are made from wood. A simple

Wooden bridge.

plank bridge can be plain or covered with pounded clay, on to which is laid moss or turf. Another version, the drum bridge, is made from sections of log laid side by side across two beams stretching from bank to bank. Often, these bridges are gracefully arched for reasons of strength as well as aestheticism.

Log bridge with turf covering – a good bridge for a rustic application.

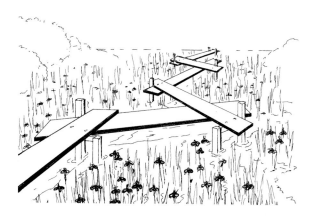

Plank bridge – planks look good over a swampy area.

There are many variations of plank bridges that fall into the semi-formal category (see the illustration above). The yatsubashi is made from eight wooden planks set at angles to one another and is very popular for crossing streams, reed beds and swampy areas.

There are some beautiful examples of semi-formal stone bridges that are simple cleanly cut beams of stone, sometimes of extraordinary length. Some of these stone beams are gracefully curved and make a poignant juxtaposition with the natural forms of trees

and water that surround them. Stone beams can also be used singly or in combinations of different lengths. Single, curved, flat-stone bridges can look good and are available imported from China.

Stone bridge – a natural block of stone makes a good bridge for a mountainous landscape.

Invariably, stones will be found at the four corners of the bridge. Depending on the character of the bridge, these stones can quite formal stone blocks, or roughly hewn stones each of different character. These are called the guardian stones and often a feature is made of them.

Guardian stones.

There are many formally shaped bridges in Japanese gardens, ranging from gentle graceful curves to the more dramatic 'drum'-shaped bridge, which is based upon a section through the traditional taiko drum. There are also some stone bridges that are made from long thin lengths of granite, but the cost of these will probably be beyond the average gardener.

Constructing Stone Bridges

Although the bridges are often decorative, they obviously need to be strong enough to take the weight of someone trying to cross them. When constructing the bridge, the foundations must be well executed. Care should be taken to set the main bridge section level, and there should be no movement when the bridge is crossed.

Before laying a stone block across a stream or gully, two pads of concrete will need to be set to take its weight. Two supporting stone blocks set upon the concrete pads are usually used to raise the bridge a good height above the water. Make sure the foundations are thoroughly hardened before attempting to set the stone, and disguise any concrete foundations when the bridge is completed.

Suitable stone can often be found in stone merchants' yards or suppliers of reclaimed building materials.

Constructing Wooden Bridges

The sections for wooden bridges should be made from sound, pressure-treated timber, with the parts bolted together with galvanized coach bolts or coach screws. To alleviate rotting of the wood, try to set the bridge's legs on to caste concrete pads. If it is necessary to set the stone or wooden legs of the bridge in the water, care should be taken to protect the pond liner. This can be achieved by preparing a concrete pad that rests on a piece of extra liner. If possible, there should be another concrete pad below the liner to stop any movement. These considerations should be taken into account at the design stage, before the pond is constructed.

Left: *Natural stone bridge.*

Above: *Stone bridge with guardian stones.*

Right: *Setting a stone bridge.*

Covered bench.

The traditional koshikake or Tea Ceremony waiting arbour can provide a quiet sheltered place to view the garden.

BENCHES AND SEATING AREAS

It is always beneficial to have a place to sit and appreciate the garden. Traditionally, this would be in the room facing the garden and the shoji screens would be drawn back to reveal the garden's beauty. Often, the main viewing place for the garden is the veranda, from where the whole composition of the landscape can be absorbed. If the seating area is to be situated actually in the garden, the 'right' place needs to be found. This may be a secluded spot – a refuge from the world – distant, and perhaps not even visible from the house.

Before deciding on the position of the seating area, walk around the garden and check the view from different positions. Just as a dog will wander around a room until it finds its own 'spot', we instinctively know our own favourite garden view. The final choice of place may have to be modified according to the needs of others and this could mean that a more formal seating area such as a porch or decking will form the main viewing place. Again, benches or seating areas should be classed as formal, semi-formal or rustic. The nearer to the house the seating area is set, the more formal the structure; the further away from the house, the more informal it should become.

In the tea garden, special arbours called koshikake are provided for guests awaiting the Tea Ceremony. Similar constructions, providing protection from wind and rain, can be made in a rustic style. Traditionally, these structures are made from clay and reed spread over a wooden frame, like the 'wattle and daub' construction of early European houses. The benches inside the koshikake waiting arbour are made of simple wooden planks. The roof supports are often carefully chosen rustic logs with the bark removed, and the roof itself can be thatched with reeds or cedar bark. Clay tiles or wooden shingles are further roofing options.

Exterior-grade plywood, or the concrete boards mentioned in the section on walls, painted with exterior paint of a sandy colour are suitable materials for constructing the walls of a copy of a koshikake.

Decking used as a transition between the house and garden.

Wooden shingles or convenient reed panels can be an alternative to the traditional thatching.

For seating in other areas, a simple bench can be made from wood, or a stone bench can be made from reclaimed materials. A stone bench looks good, but cushions may be needed to keep the cold of the stone at bay.

DECKING

Raised decking has become very popular for patios or seating areas just off the main house. This type of wooden structure softens the transition between house and garden in the way that the traditional veranda of Japanese houses does. The geometric design of decking contrasts very well with the Japanese design motifs and with the natural forms of the plantings that can be incorporated into its construction. The diagram on the opposite page shows a few decking patterns that might suit a more modern garden.

The timber used for decking should be pressure-treated with preservative, and it is best to use zinc-plated screws to screw the timber together. Any cuts in the wood should be thoroughly treated with extra wood preservative.

To help preserve the decking, the whole framework should be raised at least a few centimetres above the ground on concrete pads. Prepare the ground beneath the decking by levelling and laying a sheet of weed-suppressant membrane covered with 5cm of 20mm shingle. If a more permanent base is desired, 75mm of concrete can be laid.

LIGHTING

Lanterns

Lanterns, like fences and water basins, have become an indispensable part of the Japanese garden and an art form in their own right. Originally, lanterns were used in the religious confines of temples but were then 'borrowed' by the tea masters for use in the tea garden. From there they were taken for use in courtyard gardens and other secular situations. Today, most lanterns are made of stone, but bronze ones can be found in some temples in Japan.

Lanterns are perhaps the one thing that says 'Japanese garden' to most people, although their

Decking patterns.

A lantern and tsukubai arrangement.

Old stone lantern.

Stone lantern, Hagi, Japan.

presence in the garden is not mandatory. Care needs be taken over their placement in order to avoid creating a kitsch pastiche of a Japanese garden, but, used wisely and skilfully, they provide a design element that is very useful and difficult to replace.

The lantern should always be placed where a lantern would be needed, even if its function is purely for aesthetic reasons, otherwise it will look unbalanced and out of context. It should, therefore, be placed next to the water basin, a path or a bridge. Light the lantern, even if only occasionally, as its welcoming glow will provide an extra design dimension to the garden.

A subtle balance between the type of lantern used and the shapes of the other elements in the garden, is a very important aspect of Japanese garden design. The strong upright formality of the lantern is a good counter-balance against both the flatness of paths and the flowing natural forms of plants. Never buy a lantern just because of its pleasing

shape and then try to fit it in with other things. Look at all the other shapes involved – rocks, water basin, plants – and then buy the lantern only if it fits in with these other elements.

Many of the lantern styles that are available are based on very old temple designs, or on those developed by the main tea masters. Old lanterns are very highly valued in Japan and only occasionally change hands.

There are several groups into which lanterns can be placed. Those that sit upon their own base are called tachigata and range in height from about 1.5m to 3–4m high. Ikekomigata lanterns have their pedestals buried in the ground, range in size between 1.2m and 2.5m, and are therefore slightly less formal. The okidoro are

Oribe lantern and bamboo.   *Yamadoro lantern.*

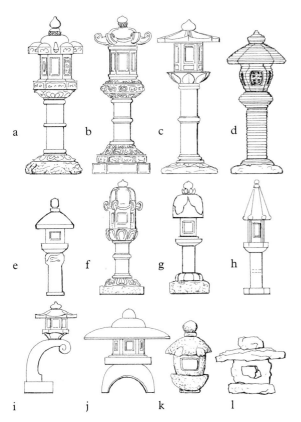

Lantern seller's yard.

Various stone lanterns: 'a' – kasuga; 'b' – kodai; 'c' – yunoki; 'd' – doufu; 'e' – oribe; 'f' – rikyu; 'g' – kyomuzou; 'h' – rengeji; 'i' – rankei; 'j' – kodai maru; 'k' – misaki; 'l' – yamadoro.

small lanterns that are easily movable, do not have a real pedestal and often sit on a flat piece of stone. They are usually placed beside a path or in places where a strong vertical element is not needed in the design.

Yukimigata are designed with a large flat top, the purpose of which is to collect snow. 'Snow viewing' is a popular pastime in Japan, as is hanami, or 'flower viewing', when people go out to see the cherry blossom in spring. Yukimigata are usually multi-legged, range in height from 40cm to 2m, and are often placed by water.

Although most forms of lantern are quite formal, there is a type called yamadoro, which is made from collected pieces of natural stone, put together to form a lantern-like shape. This type of lantern is strictly for a 'rustic' situation.

A wide variety of lanterns made from concrete, resin and various types of stone are available from suppliers. The best ones are imported from Japan and are hand-carved in a hard sandstone or granite. Slightly less expensive lanterns are available carved in granite from China, but care must be taken when choosing as the quality of the carving work varies greatly. Still cheaper ones are available from Thailand, carved in a soft black lava stone, but, again, the carving is often poor, although they do tend to 'weather down' very quickly. The concrete lanterns occasionally seen for sale in Europe also weather down quickly, but have little real presence. Resin lanterns are strictly to be avoided – they are usually quite garish in colour, and are, of course, non-functional.

Other Lighting

Lighting should be considered seriously when planning the garden. A light in the darkness not only

Misaki lantern.

*Under bridge
lighting detail.*

has a very significant, deep-seated inner resonance, but it also brings a beautiful dimension to the garden. Evening can be the most magical time to view a garden and careful lighting enhances its composition and gives it a more intimate ambience.

Lighting should not be intrusive and a naked light should never be allowed to blind the eye to the beauty of the garden. It is always best to see just the result of the light and not its source. The popular high-power halogen lamps generally used for outdoor lighting are best avoided as they flood the site with a cold blanket of light that creates stark shadows. A small spotlight revealing a water basin or a beautiful old stone in the path is much more effective, and will say more about the garden than a great flood of light will. Use light to 'explain' the garden.

Think carefully about which of the main features of the garden should be accented. Pathways may need to be illuminated, and water basins, ponds or rock groups may need to be highlighted. Attention can be drawn to differing textures and effects by illuminating a rock group in one area and foliage in another. Gravel can be effectively lit by installing a concealed light at low level and shining it across the gravel. The flat plane then seems to be washed by the light.

Low-level lighting usually works best. A light thrown up into a plant is generally more effective than a light shining down on it. However, a light set into the ground and shining up into a tree can produce beautiful results. In one client's garden there were many existing mature silver birch trees, which he wished to retain. Further trees were added to fill in gaps and create a small copse into which lamps were shone vertically up into the trees. When the leaves turn yellow in autumn, the evening garden seems to be in a golden snowstorm; it is a stunning effect that lasts for several weeks.

Outdoor lighting systems are easily installed, being almost invariably either solar-powered or of 12 volts, with a light sensor and a timer. As with pond pumps, wet weather and electricity do not make a good mix, but there are few problems with 12-volt systems and it should not be necessary to engage a professional electrician. The main problem is not with safety but with connecting the transformer to the primary source of electricity and disguising the cables. Solar-powered lights do not pose this problem.

Garden lights usually have 7-watt or 10-watt bulbs in 12-volt systems. Normally, illumination from the light will reach about 1.5m each side of the feature, but this will depend on the number of lights used, the wattage of the bulbs and the length of the cable. Fortunately, these lights are easily moved; it may be necessary to try them in several places before you get the effect you desire.

CHAPTER 5

Water Features and Water Effects

GENERAL PRINCIPLES

Japanese gardens need a correct mix of elements if they are to be balanced; consequently, no garden should ever be without water. Even the Karesansui dry stone gardens have stylized water – the name derives from *kare* ('dry' or 'withered'), *san* ('mountain'), and *sui* ('water') – represented by flat gravel ground cover. Even if it is only in the chozubachi water basin, there is always water somewhere in the Japanese garden. The movement of water has the effect of moving the air, too, which, together with a stimulating sound, enlivens the house and garden.

In the East, water is synonymous with wealth and, to be most beneficial, idealistically this wealth/water must always flow towards the house. This is a fundamental aspect of geomancy, which also links to the Buddhist ideals of purity. Geomancy is largely based on common sense, and water must not be left to stagnate as stagnant water brings disease and foul stenches.

Carefully composed reflections on water offer another dimension in the design of the garden. The Japanese often place water features where they will reflect the light of the full moon at various times of the year. One famous garden has a spring where the full moon is said to wash itself in the ripples of the water. This reflective effect can also be used to good purpose in the placement of a water basin. Remember that a pond will form a smooth visual plane against which to show off the textures of rocks and plants, and which will also bounce light into the garden.

The Japanese gardener has developed the art of manipulating water through waterfalls and watercourses into an aquatic dance of sound and movement. As well as enhancing any water feature, a waterfall has the practical element of invigorating the water in the pond. Waterfalls can be many and varied: they may be single falls or multiple falls, with levels that can be quite separate or grouped together. A variety of landscapes can be suggested by joining together differing levels of waterfall with small ponds or stretches of stream.

In the Japanese garden, a stream can be symbolic both of a river and of the passage of the human being through life. Building this feature can be therapeutic if the garden takes on the story of your life with its convoluted twists and turns, highs and lows, struggles and achievements, and dramas and quiet times. The river can become the main feature in the Japanese garden and if the story of the river explains itself convincingly to you then it will convey the feeling to others, too.

Pine over an ancient pond.

SITING THE WATER FEATURE

Having decided that you want a water feature in your garden, you need to consider several points. First, the suitability of the site must be examined. If the site is flat, there may be few problems in constructing a pond, but if it is on a slope, in a hollow, or if the water table is too high, measures will have to be taken to allow for these difficulties.

In a hollow site, rainwater may drain into the pond and, if provision is not made to remove excess water, it may flood the garden area. If your garden is on a slope, building a pond will prove technically difficult. Any leaks or flooding may cause the whole construction to slide down the slope, with disastrous consequences, especially if your house is at the bottom. On a sloping site, a more effective use of water would be to build a small stream with a series of small ponds and waterfalls, matching the pond to the geography of the site. This is also more in keeping with the way water would naturally gather and flow, and will give a more pleasing and natural design. As

in all matters of Japanese garden design, take your cue from nature.

The water table is the height below ground surface where water naturally settles and this varies according to the time of the year. If you dig a hole at the site of your pond and it rapidly fills with water, your water table may be too high for the successful creation of a pond. It might be possible to create a natural pond, but this may disappear in summer when the water table drops. Unfortunately, if you install a pond liner here, the ground water may gather under it and it could balloon up into the finished pond. Alternative water features should be considered if the water table in your garden is too high.

PONDS

Consider the kind of landscape you are creating before deciding on the shape and size of your pond. Is

Small pond in a private garden.

the pond you plan to build a representation of a seascape or is it a pond in the mountains? Will the pond be big enough to contain an island? Whatever you create, it must be suggestive of the type of landscape you have chosen to emulate. It is your pond and it must please you.

Siting and Digging the Pond

Before starting to build the pond, carefully work out how it will fit into the overall design. Look for any logistical problems you may encounter. It makes sense to move things before you start digging so, if you are going to need rocks for a feature on the far side of the pond, put them there before excavation starts. What are you going to do with the earth that has been displaced? Will it be used to bank up around the pond, can it be used in another part of the garden, or will you have to have it removed?

Is anything going to overshadow your pond? Are there trees or buildings close by? To have a pond bubbling among ferns, beneath the shade of a spreading tree, seems romantic and ethereal, but if you plan to have flowering plants such as water-lilies, these will need plenty of sunlight. Trees and buildings block out the sun very effectively. Trees give dappled shade and deciduous varieties will let more light through to the pond during winter. Buildings, however, give profound shade, which is extended during winter by the low angle of the sun. Check to see where the sun will fall on the pond at all times of the day, in both summer and winter, if possible. Siting the pond near trees causes further problems as fallen

leaves may sink to the bottom of the pond, forming a toxic mush, thereby creating methane gas, which can prove fatal to fish. For some methods to counteract such problems, see pages 134–5.

When you have decided where to put your pond, the next thing to consider is how it will be dug. Unless your pond is fairly small, digging by hand may turn out to be a bigger task than you imagine. Hiring a Bobcat or similar small, tracked digger might be the answer, but think carefully about your access to the site. Wide drives may be ideal, but the side passageways of townhouses are often very narrow, with restricted access. If you do have access for a JCB, it may be most economical to hire both the machine and a driver to dig the pond. Big machinery can shift a lot of soil and achieve a great deal in just a few hours. However, even if you use a machine, you will still have to finish the digging by hand, to get the correct gradients on its sides and to incorporate any shelves for baskets of water plants.

Constructing the Pond

The traditional way of constructing a pond in Japan, as in Europe, is to line it with pounded clay. This can still be done, but is very hard work and quite expensive, unless there is plenty of suitable clay on site. There are several other less arduous and less expensive ways to construct a pond.

Flexible liners are ideal for creating irregularly shaped ponds, and are by far the best choice for the DIY gardener. They are also the choice of most professionals as they are the quickest and most

Pond lined with stone.

Large pond under construction.

economical to install. PVC liners are cheapest, but only have a maximum life expectancy of ten years. Butyl liners are more expensive but will last twenty to fifty years, depending on quality and thickness. A less expensive alternative to Butyl is a new type of PVC liner called 'Hi-lastic', which can now be found in most water-garden centres.

A Butyl liner can be used for the construction of quite a large pond, but it would have to be specially ordered, as several sections would need to be welded together. Also, a very large liner may need to be unloaded by crane. It is possible to weld some liners on site, but this is usually only considered for big, professional projects. A recent innovation, developed for reservoirs, is to line the pond with a thin, strong membrane, which is then sandwiched between layers of sand. For very large ponds, this 'sandwich' is easier to fit than Butyl. Butyl's black colour is visually very good, but care must be taken to hide the liner at the sides of the pond and in any shallow areas.

Concrete can also be utilized, and has an excellent texture that is seldom matched by other liners. This method tends to be used more on formal shapes. A reinforcing mesh is sandwiched between layers of waterproofed concrete and, in large ponds, is usually cast in sections with wooden shuttering moulds. The overall dimensions of the excavated hole will have to be slightly larger to account for the thickness of the reinforced concrete sandwich. The process of laying the concrete really requires expert handling, especially if the pond is of any great size.

On some sites, both concrete and Butyl are used in pond construction, with the material being chosen depending on the nature of the shapes in the design.

Concrete can be laid in a more formal shape and then rock may be built into it after the initial shape has been set. Great care must be taken to make sure that the pond is sealed and no water can escape behind rocks. Chemicals in the concrete can be neutralized and it will discolour with time and algal growth, and become more visually pleasing. A more professional look can be obtained by covering the raw concrete with a black paint-on coating, which is safe to fish and plants. However, if you intend to keep fish, the lime in the concrete must be neutralized by one method or another.

Pre-cast shapes in plastic or fibreglass are easy to fit, but not really suitable for the Japanese garden as they look artificial and are unlikely to fit into the basic overall design.

Shaping the Pond

Ponds in Japanese gardens take many traditional shapes – a heart, a snake, a kidney or even a sweet potato – but an abstract amorphous shape also works well. The widest part of the pond should be towards the house as it provides a sense of perspective and depth across the plane of the water. Another trick of perspective often used is to obscure one side of the pond with some planting in the foreground. When observed from the main viewing place, this has the visual effect of suggesting that the expanse of water is bigger than it is by tricking the eye into thinking that

Setting out the shape using a garden hose.

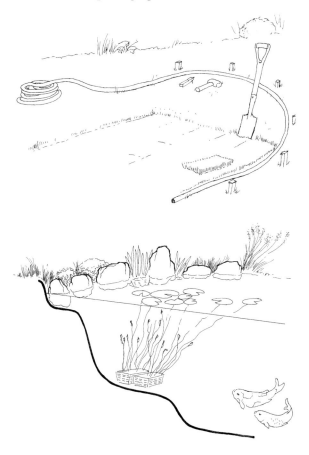

Pond section showing deep area for fish in winter.

the pond extends for some distance behind the planting.

When you have selected the site, size and shape of your pond, set it out to check that it harmonizes with other aspects of the design. A garden hose laid out on the ground is a good tool to use in getting the shape right. Some small change in shape will nearly always be made to improve the design when the liner is fitted.

The depth of your pond will depend on what you want to put in it. If you want to keep fish, 50–60cm is the minimum feasible depth, although it will not need to be this deep everywhere. If you want to keep Koi carp, or if you live in an area that is prone to prolonged freezing, you will probably need an area in the pond that is 1m deep. Having a good depth also helps keep the water cool and clear.

Koi carp, Rakusho Kisaten, Kyoto.

If you plan to keep fish, or grow plants in your pond, it is vital for the pond to have a variety of depths to accommodate the needs of different varieties of plant or species of fish. This can be achieved by incorporating into your design shelves that can be set at differing heights. Shelving provides a place to stand marginal plants in baskets, a means by which amphibious creatures can get out of the pond more easily, and shallower water where fish can spawn. It also eliminates some of the stress problems that arise with straight-sided pools, which should only be of a rigid construction. If you are using a flexible liner, and shelves are not incorporated, it is important that the sides of the pond do not go straight down, but slope at a slight angle (20 degrees to the vertical is ideal).

Camouflaging the Edges

Whatever type, size or shape of liner you use, it is important from a visual aspect that the edges are camouflaged in an appropriate way. This should be considered before you start digging.

Disguising the edges of a pond can be the most difficult part of its construction. As the liner must rise above the water level to prevent seepage, careful thought must be given to how this camouflage can be achieved. The work you do at the edges will affect the whole appearance of the pond, and dictate how natural it looks when finished. One way of achieving a natural look is to set small pieces of rock in

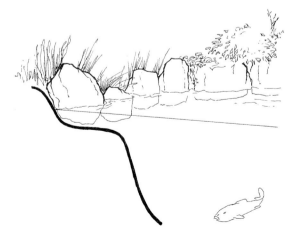

Pond liner with the edge obscured by rocks covering the edges.

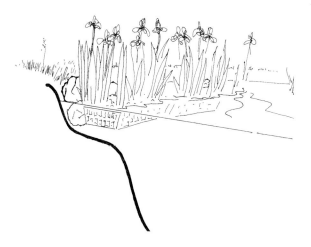

Pond liner hidden by shelf with plants.

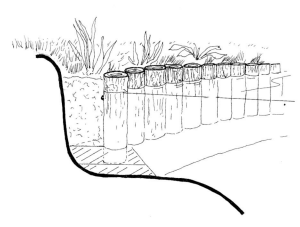

Edge hidden by logs set in concrete with planting behind.

waterproofed cement at the edges of the pond. Alternatively, a shelf can be set at about 30cm below the proposed surface; marginal plants, such as irises, can be grown in baskets on this in order to obscure the edge from sight. (See Chapter 6 for more on plants and planting.)

If you are designing a seascape, some areas at the edges of the pond may represent beaches. This is easily achieved with the use of cobblestones. Many stone merchants and garden centres stock graded cobbles, so you can choose the size of cobble that suits the scale of your beach. What you are creating is just a representation; the shape of the area is what makes the eye recognize it as a beach. You do not need

to use sand, which would be very difficult to maintain. Cobbles are ideal, as they are smooth, and unlikely to slip into the pond unless really disturbed.

The transition between water and garden can be softened by incorporating a trough-like area into the sides of the pond that can also be used for growing marginal plants.

The traditional way to finish a clay-lined pond was to hammer logs into the ground using a wood that did not rot easily. A similar effect can be achieved with logs set in a concrete trough (see the illustration at top right on the opposite page).

A steep-sided pond can be disguised by building up an inner wall of stone. This inner wall of rocks is

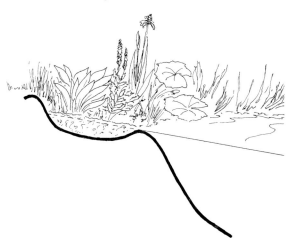

Edge hidden by boggy area and planting.

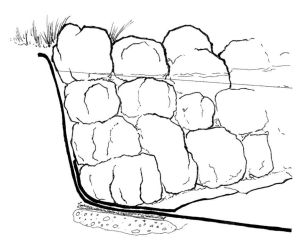

Side of pond disguised by rock wall.

Pond edge.

assembled with waterproof cement and must recline slightly backwards (see the illustration at bottom right on the opposite page). For stability, it is built on a prepared pad of concrete, which is set at the bottom of the pond below the liner. This concrete pad will need a layer of padding material over it to ensure that the liner will not be punctured. Further spare pieces of liner will have to be placed over the main liner for protection before the rockwork is constructed.

Strive to make a believable landscape. If it is meant to represent a sea or a dark mysterious pool, try to make it as natural as possible. Vary the shapes of the sides of the pond, use shallow areas and steep areas, rocky areas and areas of soft planting. If it tells a convincing story it will communicate that to other people. Nature is seldom symmetrical.

The gentler slopes in the shallows of the pond can be finished with a covering of flint cobbles or very coarse gravel. Always choose stones carefully and exclude any with sharp edges. The very bottom of the pond will quickly get a covering of detritus and, if necessary, a few carefully placed rocks will camouflage the liner there. A layer of stone-free soil can be placed over the liner if you are planning to have a wildlife-type pond. The soil will make the water muddy initially, but this soon clears. Do not use peat, as it has a tendency to float on the surface and stains the water brown.

Fitting a Flexible Liner

The size of liner you need will be the length of the pond plus twice the maximum depth of the pond by

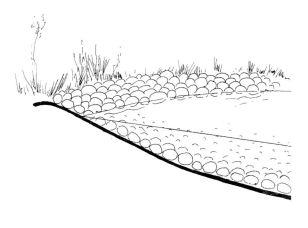

Liner obscured by cobbles.

its width plus twice its maximum depth. If you are using a Butyl liner, do not forget to take account of the area above the water line when calculating the size to order. If it is within your budget, it might be wise to order extra liner to account for unforeseen problems. Pieces can be joined on afterwards if necessary, but the join will never be a hundred per cent successful; the cost of trying to solve leaks far outweighs the cost of an extra bit of liner. Off-cuts can usually be used for packing under rocks or for extra protection anywhere that the liner is vulnerable, so nothing need be wasted.

If you are using a Butyl liner, have it waiting on site so that it is ready to install when the digging is completed. After the shape is formed, it is a good idea to go over the area meticulously and remove any

Installing a huge liner.

stones that may cause damage to the liner. Remember that there will be a tremendous pressure on it when it is filled with water. Prior to installing a liner, you can cover the base of the pond with about 5cm of soft sand, to minimize the possibility of perforation by stones. It is also advisable to lay polyester matting under the liner as extra protection; this should be available from the liner's supplier. Fibreglass loft-insulating material, available from any DIY store, is also suitable for this purpose.

Check again that all the edges of the pond are at the same height. Water finds its own level and any height differences in the sides of the pond will be accentuated, and the liner made visible. Major faults are quite difficult to correct once the pond is full of water, but minor differences are correctable and bound to occur as the ground settles. If your pond is of small to medium size, a plank of wood can be placed from side to side across the top, or across the corners, and a spirit level placed on the plank to ascertain any differences in level that might have occurred during digging. Most professionals use a transparent polythene tube filled with water. Wherever you place the two ends of the tube the water will be the same height, and you can check the level all round.

Only when you are sure that the pond is the size and shape that you desire and that the sides are level, and you have decided on your edging materials, you can start to install the liner. Prior to installation, lay the liner out in the sun for a while if possible, as this will render it a little more pliable and make the task easier. Carefully arrange the liner over the excavated hole, checking the fit around any areas of complex shape. If the pond is large, and you have to get inside, be very careful and walk on a piece of sacking, carpet or an off-cut placed on top of the liner. As you work around the pond, arranging the liner according to the maker's instructions, it may pay to lay a few bricks on any part of the liner that has folds.

Once the liner has been fitted over the whole shape, any areas where edging work is to be built can be completed before the pond is filled. Again, do not forget to use extra protection from off-cuts or under-felt where appropriate. Use a proprietary water roofer in the cement used around rockwork and then add some mortar colourant to blend it in with the rock colour. Any built-in pipes needed for filling or drainage should be incorporated at this point. Install any edge treatments and lay cobbles or gravel to disguise shallow areas of liner. Try to foresee any places where the liner might become visible before you start filling, as it might be difficult to correct afterwards.

If you wish to keep fish in a small pond, it will need to be virtually the same depth as a large pond; this can be a problem, as there may be so many folds in the liner that it will be difficult to fit. If your pond is of a smaller size (3 x 2m or less), and the edging can be completed after the pond has been filled, an alternative method of fitting the liner can be used.

Make sure that there are no sharp stones anywhere in the pond area and take the same precautions to protect the liner as you would when making a large pond. The liner is equally vulnerable whatever its size. If the liner has a light side and a dark side (black), remember to use it with the dark side uppermost.

The liner, having warmed in the sun, should be draped over the hole so that it dips into it and touches the base. The liner should then be weighted around the edges with heavy stones; this will anchor it and prevent it slipping into the pond under the weight of the water during filling. As the pond is slowly filled with water, the liner will slightly stretch and mould itself closely to the contours of the pond. As the weight of water increases and more liner is needed, relieve the stress on the liner by shifting some of the anchor stones, allowing the liner to slip slightly. Some folds will still occur, but they can be minimized by tugging the liner's edges to make sure that it lies as straight as possible.

When the pond has been filled, any excess material can be trimmed away and the pond can be edged to fit in with your overall design.

Concrete Ponds

Concrete is most useful for formal ponds because of its rigidity, but that rigidity also makes it vulnerable to cracking. The effects of ice, shifting soil and subsidence can lead to irreparable damage that might make anyone wonder why they considered the material in the first place. Large concrete ponds need very careful planning and are often best left to a professional to complete, as the consequences of making mistakes on this scale can be catastrophic. However, concrete is inexpensive and does have a pleasing texture that cannot be matched by flexible liners.

If the pond is in an area that is prone to prolonged freezing, the possibility of cracking may be minimized by having sloping sides; ice can then move upwards as it expands. This may reduce the volume of water in the pond but it will also reduce some of the stresses.

Details of suitable concrete mixes and fixing shuttering can be found in most DIY manuals. The main thing to remember when making a concrete pond is the vital importance of having readied everything that you are going to need for its completion before you begin. Preparation is paramount and there can be no short cuts if it is to be successful. It is not a job that can be left halfway through while you find more materials. Even if the pond has sloping walls, not only will the concrete require shuttering that has to be fixed in stages as sections harden, but it will also require reinforcement with wire mesh before a second layer of concrete can be added.

A Butyl liner can last up to fifty years, is easier to fit, can easily be disguised and is not prone to cracking. Concrete ponds cause a great deal of hard work for what amounts to a minimal aesthetic improvement.

Filling and Emptying the Pond

If you are using a flexible liner, put heavy rocks on the top overlapping edges of the liner to ensure that there is no slippage and then gradually fill the pond with water, easing out as many wrinkles in the liner as possible as you progress. Cut off the extra liner only after the pond is completely filled and you are satisfied with its shape. You can now complete your remaining edge treatments to obscure any visible liner.

It is a good idea to leave the pond filled overnight and then to pump the water out and refill it with fresh water. This will remove chemicals from the cement used for the rockwork or edging. If you intend to keep fish, this process may need to be repeated several times in order to eliminate any residual lime. Alternatively, cemented areas can be treated with a silicate that will neutralize the lime; the water should then need to be replaced only once. It is best if the final fill is with rainwater. Tapwater contains dissolved salts and minerals, on which the dreaded blanket weed thrives, and is one of the causes of greening of pondwater in summer.

If your pond is large, baskets holding deep-water plants such as water-lilies can be positioned at the bottom of the pond just before filling takes place. (See Chapter 6 for more details on plants and planting.) Oxygenating plants and any other plants can be installed after filling, but fish should not be put in for several weeks, until the whole system has settled down. Four weeks might be an appropriate length of time to wait, but this can be shortened with the use of proprietary brands of water conditioners.

Evaporation will always cause some loss of water from the pond; the amount will vary from day to day with the weather conditions. A dry, windy day can strip moisture from a large expanse of water at an amazing rate, so some means of topping up must be installed. If the pond is small, a garden hose can occasionally be used to refill it after any loss. If it is large, it will be more effective to install a permanent connection.

The best way to make a permanent connection is to build a chamber from pre-cast concrete manhole rings, or to use a pre-formed plastic manhole. The manhole should be as close to the edge of the pond as possible, but obscured from view. The pond and manhole are connected by a fixed pipe or trough (see the illustration below), and set so that the desired level of water in the pond corresponds with the level of water in the manhole. A water supply is brought into the manhole and terminated in a ball valve that is set so that it shuts off when the correct level is reached, but comes on when the level drops.

If the pond is in a hollow, rainwater could easily flood surrounding land or cause land slippage if it is close to a slope. These factors may have been taken into consideration when the pond was planned. If not, provision should be made for getting rid of the excess rainwater. If a storm drain is available, one method of drainage is to connect the pond to it using a pipe that should incline slightly towards the drain from just above the pond's water level. The mouth of the pipe should be covered with wire mesh to prevent the pipe becoming blocked by debris. This mesh will need regular checking to ensure that it also remains clear of debris and does not become choked itself. If a storm drain is not available near by, it may be necessary to dig a soakaway. For a pond up to 50 square metres, this should consist of a hole of about 1 square metre, filled with rubble or old stone, and connected to the pond via a pipe set just at water level. Overflowing water will gradually seep into the hole and filter out into the surrounding soil.

Periodically, the pond will need to undergo maintenance and cleaning, and will have to be emptied. For a small pond that has a pump fitted, the pipe from the pump can be disconnected, and the water can be pumped out into the drain or soakaway. In a large rigid pond, it may pay to fit a drain valve in the bottom of the pond to take the water to a convenient drain. If a drain valve is fitted, it is important that any drained water is taken to a drainage system. If the water simply soaks into the surrounding area, it will cause erosion under the pond that will lead to structural damage. (See pages 134–5, on pond maintenance.)

Safety

If safety is a potential problem with your pond, steel mesh resting on welded supports, which sit on concrete pads, can be installed just below the surface of the water. Concrete reinforcing mesh is suitable for this purpose but great care must be taken not to puncture the liner during installing. The mesh should only be visible if you are looking straight down on to it. It will not be visible at an angle because of the reflection of the sky and will still present a clear flat plane of water to the viewer.

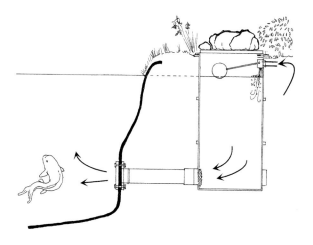

A refill chamber constructed from a plastic manhole unit with a ball valve fitted.

Pumps

There are many design ideas for bringing water into the pond: a waterfall, spring, or even a small stream might terminate in the pond. However, if any of these methods are chosen, installation of a water pump will be necessary to circulate the water, and provision will have to be made to bring both power and water to the site.

There are two types of water pump available: the dry surface-mounted pump and the submersible pump. Surface-mounted pumps are most suited to very large water features with high waterfalls that require great water pressure. Submersible pumps are suitable for most garden designs, and are convenient and easy to install. An acceptable installation for a small pond of up to 30 square metres is for a submersible pump to sit near the bottom of the pond disguised by a few loose rocks. The pump should be slightly raised on blocks to ensure that none of the detritus in the bottom of the pond is sucked into the pump.

A better solution for a larger pond is to build a pump chamber. This chamber can be constructed in the same way as the ball valve chamber. A direct connection between the manhole and the pond is required, allowing water to flood the bottom of the chamber. The pump is set into the water, which is then drawn up and pumped out through flexible piping to the water feature (see above).

When deciding which size pump will be needed, the size of the pond, the diameter of the pipe that will supply the feature, the length of the pipe and also the characteristics of the feature must be taken into account. If the pump is to supply a waterfall, the height to which the pump must raise the water – referred to as the head height – and the amount of water going over the falls must be considered. A pump that delivers a large volume at low pressure is usually more useful than one that delivers at high pressure. High-pressure pumps are more suitable for fountains.

It is always better to get a pump with more capacity than you need. The rate of flow can be adjusted by fitting a stopcock, but it cannot be increased above its maximum capacity. The flow of water could be divided with water being pumped both to the head of a waterfall and to falls at a lower level. An impressively built waterfall should have more than a mere trickle of water coming over it. However, the pump output per hour should not exceed the overall

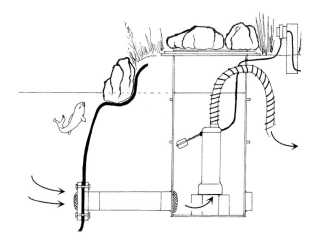

A pump chamber constructed from a plastic manhole unit.

capacity of the pond. A rate of 1,500 litres per hour will normally give a curtain of water about 15cm wide. If the water feature is extensive, and a surface-based unit is required, the pump will need to be placed near the pond within a ventilated chamber that has easy access for maintenance.

Noise is another feature that needs to be considered. Submersible pumps are quiet because they are under the water; surface-mounted pumps tend to be noisy. A Japanese garden is a place of peace and tranquillity that should not be disturbed by excessive noise from a water pump.

Electricity will be needed to work the pump and a supply provision must be made at a convenient place. Installing an electricity supply is not a job for an amateur, and, as the installation must comply with all safety regulations, a qualified electrician should be employed. Low-voltage (12-volt) pumps are available, but they have a tendency to be low in power, and are usable only for very small features. Pumps suitable for most features are generally mains-operated and should be professionally installed.

Electricity and water do not mix well, so all materials used must be both waterproof and weatherproof, with a circuit breaker as an extra safety precaution. As a protection against accidental damage and frost damage, both electric cables and water pipes need to be at least 30cm below the surface of the ground. A depth of 50–60cm is adequate in all but the severest weather conditions. To cause as little disturbance as possible, plan carefully so that all trenches are dug and cables are laid before any planting takes place.

An outdoor weatherproof socket is usually best installed close to the pump so that the supply can easily be disconnected during maintenance and cleaning. It may be convenient for the electricity supply switch to be located inside the house, so that the pump can be switched on and off at will. A timer can be useful to give regular supply for water circulation and is easily fitted.

Filtration Systems

Filtration systems are not generally needed but may be essential if you plan to have Koi carp, to keep the water sweet. Consult your fish supplier about the minimum requirements of water quality.

Filters fall generally into two types, both of which rely on the use of a pump. Most commonly, they work simply by filtering out particles in water, and drawing them through a filter attached to a pump. The others work biologically on fish waste and debris through the growth of micro-organisms that flourish within the filter itself. Biological filters, which are best kept separate from the pool, as they have a tendency to be rather unattractive and bulky, can take several months to establish and should be kept running in all but the most severe weather conditions.

It is possible to build a natural filtration system for your fish, especially if you have a long length of stream that feeds the pond. If the stream passes through various small ponds with aquatic plants and gravel beds, the water system will purify itself. It may take a while to settle down but, as the system maintains itself, it will not incur the running costs or the maintenance problems of an electricity powered filtration system.

WATERFALLS

General Principles

When designing a waterfall, keep in mind the relative heights and widths of each fall. To bring movement and realism to the feature, they should never be equal; this is a fundamental tenet of Japanese design. Try to make the rock arrangements look as natural as

possible. There is no substitute for taking a few days' holiday and going up into the mountains to study how nature does it; even making a few sketches will stimulate a flood of ideas.

Many different types of waterfall can be incorporated into your design. A single very narrow fall may suggest a huge waterfall or cataract when it is seen from a distance. This type of fall is associated with mountainous landscapes and is usually used in parts of the garden that are meant to simulate

Unequal falls – a dramatic waterfall supplied by two channels at different heights.

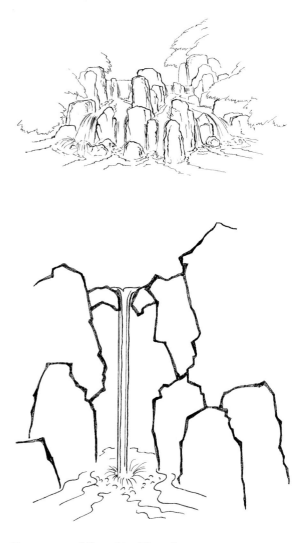

Cataract waterfall – a thin ribbon of water suggests great height.

mountainous regions. Often it is the fall that is highest and furthest away of a group of falls. In nature, the speed of a river slows as it passes through flatter, more gentle countryside, where the waterfalls become shallower and wider.

Cascade falls tend to be a series of related falls, one after another, where the ground is quite steeply sloping. The flow of water over the individual elements is fast but not very dramatic, but the whole series together makes a very impressive scene. Another splendid effect can be achieved by water falling through chutes in single and multiple combinations; again, they are often not very high, but they are impressive.

When water falls over a flat stone, it forms a curtain fall. The curtain can be single, with the rock cut away behind it, or it can be broken into two or more smaller curtains. For multiple curtain falls, the individual curtains of water should be of unequal width, to be in accord with Japanese design principles.

Pleasing visual and aural effects can be achieved as water from the fall lands in the pond. It can descend in a very fast chute or curtain, and splash and bubble up in what is called a 'bridal veil', or it can be broken by rocks that have 'fallen' to the bottom of the falls. Different splashing patterns and sounds can be achieved, depending on the shape and heights of these fallen rocks.

A cascading waterfall – a waterfall that cascades over a broken rocky ledge.

A narrow curtain waterfall.

Curtain falls – a fine curtain of water.

Divided curtain falls – curtain falls split by protrusions at the point where the water falls.

When planning to build a waterfall, decisions must be made about how the individual elements will fit together, how each element will be sealed against leakage, and which shape of rock will give the fall pattern you desire.

Further Design Considerations

The flow of water through the pump has to be taken into consideration when designing waterfalls. As water is pumped to the top of a waterfall, the action of the pump may cause the water to pulse from the pipe rather than proceed in a continuous flow. A small pond or holding tank above the waterfall will help to even out the flow. Stones strategically placed in the

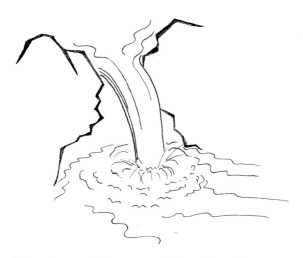

Water chute-type falls – a powerful chute of water between narrow rocks.

tank can also break up the pulsating effect. If the pump is particularly powerful, the holding tank should be as large as is possible within the design. A small pond just behind a fall will also help even out the flow of water over the 'water-falling stone'.

If only a small cataract-type fall is desired at the top of a water feature, it may be wise to split the flow of water from the pump and bring part of the flow into the fall at another level. The redirected water can enter a lower section, or even the bottom pond, depending on the impression you want to create.

Testing the flow of water will help you plan and construct the waterfall more accurately. This can be achieved quite simply by connecting up the pump, either in the completed pond or a large tank, and watching how the water emerges. In view of the fact that height affects the water flow, place the pipe at the same height as the top of the planned waterfall. Try directing the flow over variously shaped rocks to see what the flow is like and what patterns are achieved. With experience you will develop a feel for the way water flows from various pumps and waterfalls, but no two waterfalls are the same, and some fine tuning always needs to be done once everything is working.

Constructing a Waterfall

To minimize water loss from the waterfall, it is often best to lay pieces of Butyl liner into each section and overlap them to create each element. Rockwork can

Shallow falls.

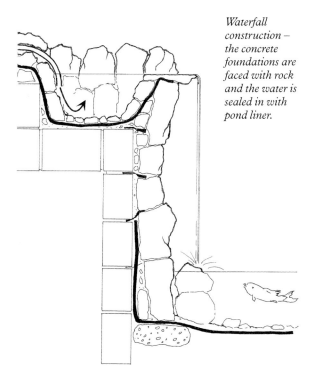

Waterfall construction – the concrete foundations are faced with rock and the water is sealed in with pond liner.

Above: *Foundations for a waterfall.*

Below: *The completed waterfall.*

then be built on top of the liner, making sure that it comes up high enough to enclose the sections when they are full of water, and that there are no sharp edges that will puncture it. Watch out for possible areas where there will be splashing, as water will be lost from the system and may cause damage by washing away surrounding earth.

Most waterfalls will require a solid foundation, and some building work will be necessary. If the waterfalls are small, this can be constructed from brickwork, but if the waterfalls are large, concrete blockwork may be needed. Building the whole feature from rock may be prohibitively expensive, so visible rock is placed on a hidden brick foundation.

As the foundation work is installed, some stainless-steel wall ties will have to be set to hold the facing rockwork in place. These ties are available from any builders' merchant and are the same as those used in general building work to link outer brickwork to inner blockwork walls.

Stones and gravel can be laid into the small ponds and stream sections to hide any liner that is still visible. Clear silicone mastic can be used to fix any small stones where a cement join would be visible;

this should not be necessary if cement colours are used in the mortar mix. Rocks can be placed to alter the direction of flow of water in the stream sections or even as it falls over the 'water-falling stone'.

STREAMS

In the Japanese garden, a stream can be symbolic both of a river and of the passage of a human being through life, and can become the garden's main feature.

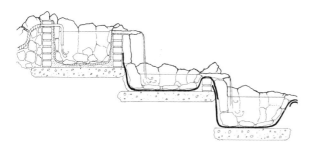

Constructing a series of waterfalls – each section can be constructed as a separate chamber with different characteristics.

Large stream.

Building this feature can be therapeutic if the garden takes on the story of your life with its convoluted twists and turns. The story of the river should explain itself convincingly to you, and to others.

In mountainous regions, streams tend to flow through deep gorges and rapids on a course that is fast and often quite straight. As the surrounding countryside becomes flatter, the stream widens to become a river that wanders as the flow slows. Eventually, the river follows a typical meandering pattern as it passes through flood plains before discharging into the sea. This termination at the sea is often characterized by a delta where the river is forced to give up its silt. In the mountains, the force of the water is so great that it can cut through the strongest rock, but in the lower regions, as the force diminishes, water tends to divert around hard obstacles such as rock, and instead erodes softer rocks and clays. This is the river story that you are trying to convey in a convincing way. To be successful in the

Narrow stream.

overall garden design, the stream needs to flow in as natural a way as possible.

Study the way that streams look in nature. The bed of a stream is a complex pattern of silt, gravel and stones. The speed of the water flowing along the stream determines the coarseness or fineness of the structure of the stream bed. Fine particles are carried in the water and deposited when an obstacle such as a rock is encountered. The very fine particles are deposited on the inside banks of river bends where the flow of water is slower. The outer banks of the river bends tend to get undercut as the current flows faster and carries larger particles that hasten erosion. These natural features can all be represented in the garden stream by using small quantities of different-sized stones and gravel, and laying them in bands on the bed of the stream. Placing rocks in the stream to divide its flow also creates interest and is very much a

A shallow meandering stream.

Construction of a large stream.

characteristic of mountain rapids.

When designing a stream for the garden, check how much fall there will be over the whole length of its proposed route. If the stream is flowing down a hill, you will be able to have contrasting flows, with sections where the flow is quite fast, and other, slower areas. If there is not much fall in the garden, you will need to make a head of the stream by mounding earth or creating a raised 'mountain' or rock structure. Only a slight fall is needed to get the water moving, and sections of the stream can be accelerated by restricting the flow with extra rocks. A fall showing about half a bubble on a spirit level is enough to give flow to water.

The site should be marked out, using string or garden hose, as for a pond. When the shape looks right, mark it with short wooden stakes. Dig out the stream where necessary and prepare the surface by removing any stones. Again, Butyl liner is often the best material to use in the construction of the sections of stream; remember to protect the liner with 5cm of soft sand and some polyester fleece. Take care that there is enough depth in the stream and that enough liner is left on the sides to allow for the rise in water level when the pump is on. If possible, it is better to leave the sides unfinished

until the stream is working, so that any unforeseen depth problems can be corrected.

The stream will look better if you design each section so that some water remains in it when the pump is switched off. This can be achieved by just slightly raising the outgoing lip so that water will only flow over it when the surge comes from the pump (see the illustration at bottom right on page 83). To create extra interest, try to connect each section of the stream in a slightly different way. Little waterfalls or chutes make nice transition features.

Plants tend to grow along the banks of a river where it flows through flatter landscapes. Areas where marginal plants can grow can be incorporated into

Stream construction – water remains in each section of the stream when the pump is turned off.

Water over pebbles.

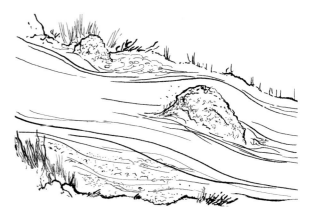

Above: *Stream flows – water rushes past a boulder in the flow.*

Below: *A spring.*

the bank of your stream by leaving the liner wider at various points, so that shallow earth- and gravel-filled pockets can be created in which plants can grow. These can be arranged so that water only enters them when the stream level rises as the pump is turned on.

SPRINGS

Springs are symbolic of the source of life, or refreshment of a worn-out spirit, and are excellent as filling points for ponds. A spring bubbling out from beneath rocks is quite easy to create and is a good way to hide the flexible hose coming from a pump. The only problem normally encountered is that the flow from a big pump is quite violent. This can be overcome to some extent either by using a

Stream flows – study the way water flows when constructing your stream.

small low-voltage pump or by having the spring as part of a larger feature. Alternatively, build a small brick chamber and direct the flow from the pipe back on itself. This tends to break up any pulsating effect created in the water flow by the pump, and the water will flow from the front of the chamber in a more convincing manner. Plants naturally grow around sources of water and this is a good way to disguise any building work.

WATER EFFECTS IN DRY GARDENS

Dry Ponds

The basic design principles of dry ponds are the same as those for wet ponds. They must be

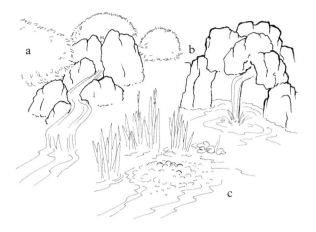

Springs: 'a' – water emerges from between rocks; 'b' – water spouts from rocks at the edge of the pond; 'c' – water bubbles up from a submerged spring.

A dry pond.

convincing. A clear distinction needs to be made between the pond and its surroundings, with edge treatments that are clearly defined. Copying the look of the wet pond, small logs can be hammered into the ground around the edge of the dry pond to good effect. Usually, the logs need only protrude 10cm above the ground level, but this would generally depend on the scale of the pond.

Usually, dry ponds do not have as much planting around them, as the impression sought is of a more austere mood, with the rock groupings being the main feature. Low clipped bushes echoing the shapes of rocks, and low-growing alpines are

Log edging defines the islands of a dry garden.

usually planted in dry-pond gardens.

The impression to be created with a dry pond, using a gravel bed, is that of a plane of water. Water is always flat, so, before constructing the pond, all turf growing on the site needs to be eliminated, the site must be levelled and any excess soil removed. Allow for a depth of 5–10cm of gravel; if there is any chance that the area will not drain easily, a 10–cm layer of crushed rubble will need to be laid below the gravel. To suppress the growth of weeds, a layer of Mypex or similar woven plastic sheet should be placed below the gravel. Even if weed seeds root into the gravel, they are easily removed if this membrane is incorporated, and any rainfall will easily disperse through its fine holes. Any rock groupings or planting should be done after the membrane is laid, but before the gravel is spread. Try to use gravel in a colour that harmonizes with any rocks that may have been used. Crushed granite of 10–14mm goes well with most rocks and is available from all stone merchants.

Dry Waterfalls

Waterfalls are often represented in the dry stone garden. The 'water' flowing over the falls is represented by coarse gravel or small cobblestones. This allows beautiful and elaborate 'waterfalls' to be created without any water being used.

Again, the design and building principles are the same as those for wet waterfalls. Some foundation work may be necessary, to support the visible rockwork. Weed-suppressant mesh should again be laid below any gravel areas. Do not forget that, when it rains, water may run down a stone fall, and precautions may need to be made to disperse any excess.

Dry Streams

Dry streams can look very dramatic when incorporated into dry landscape gardens. Stones used to form the 'river' can suggest its movement and speed. Large cobblestones suggest the more violent

Small dry waterfall.

Dry waterfall: the falling water is suggested by lines in the rocks and the 'bubbling' pebbles.

parts of the flow, while finer stones represent gentler areas. Rocks can be set into the 'flow' of the stone stream, with small cobblestones placed around the rocks creating a rushing bubbling effect as if it were moving, and the stones were rushing past them.

If the stones are convincingly placed, the effect is so realistic that it is easy to imagine the sound of bubbling water. Another effect that is often used is the construction of the dry river from flat stones laid one upon the other, like the scales of a fish. Rounded pieces of slate collected from riverbeds, and referred to by some stone merchants as 'paddle stones', are useful for this purpose. A similar effect can be created by placing flat stones on their edges and setting them in mortar over a light concrete base. The base for such a dry stream should be 50–100mm of concrete, with the stones either being set in mortar or just loosely placed. All the stones should run the same way, to give shape and direction to the flow.

Dry stream.

Stone flows: layered stone suggests the flow of water in this dry garden.

A water basin in a moss garden.

Water Basins

Water basins, or chozubachi, are another feature of Japanese gardens that have undergone the same creative revolution as fences and lanterns. The variety of their size and shape is unlimited. Originally used as

A water basin in an entranceway.

part of Buddhist purification rituals in temples, the water basin has made the same transition into the tea garden as the stone lantern. It kept its formative use in purification rituals, but became an integral part of the Tea Ceremony preparation. Later, when the artefacts of the tea garden made the transition into the secular space of the courtyard garden, the water basin became more of an abstract design element. It brought with it the design dimension of movement and freshness that any water in the garden has, however, together with the stone lantern and the stepping-stones, it was one of the three key elements for many courtyard arrangements.

Water basins also fall into the design styles of formal, semi-formal and informal or rustic. Many

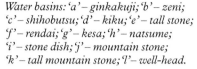

Water basins: 'a' – ginkakuji; 'b' – zeni;
'c' – shihobutsu; 'd' – kiku; 'e' – tall stone;
'f' – rendai; 'g' – kesa; 'h' – natsume;
'i' – stone dish; 'j' – mountain stone;
'k' – tall mountain stone; 'l' – well-head.

famous water basins are, in fact, reclaimed stone artefacts; objects such as column bases, large stone mortars or even naturally occurring hollowed stones have been used.

The shapes of many of the stone basins are derived from other objects. Water basins have been inspired by Chinese coins, chrysanthemums, lotus flowers, and kimono sleeves, among other things. Any receptacle can form a water basin, which need not necessarily be made of specially carved stone. Many are made of bronze or pottery, while some are simple wooden buckets.

Tsukubai

It is a common mistake to refer to a water basin as tsukubai. In fact, tsukubai is the whole arrangement of a water basin and its surrounding four stones, the yakuishi. To the front of the basin is a large flat stone on which to stand to keep the feet out of any mud. A squat stone, upon which a hand-held lantern can be placed, is found to the right of the basin. To the left is a stone on which is placed a bowl of hot water for washing the hands. To the back of the basin is placed a larger stone, to give a balance to the arrangement, and to create a

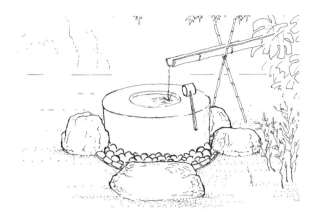

Tsukubai: the arrangement of a water basin, or chozubachi, and surrounding yakuishi stones.

composition of five elements. Uneven numbers are a fundamental of Japanese design; in this case, the four stones and the basin adhere to the principle.

Beneath the tsukubai there should be a drain system or soakaway to take spilled water from the chozubachi. Sometimes, this drain system incorporates an echo chamber called suikinkutsu, which amplifies the sound of trickling water when the water basin is used. This is a useful device to extend the design dimension and bring the element of sound into the garden.

A suikinkutsu is easily constructed using a large pot turned upside down. Two holes need to be drilled into the pot (see diagram page 90). Drill a circle of holes and then very carefully tap out the centre. On an earthenware pot, this can be done with a masonry drill, but if the pot is made of stoneware, it will be difficult to drill and you may need a diamond-tipped hole cutter. A local stonemason will probably be able to do this for you, and give it a professional finish.

The dimensions of the hole must be such that the top of the pot is flush with the ground when it is set on a supporting concrete base. The pot is then placed

Tsukubai and lantern. Nitobe tea garden.

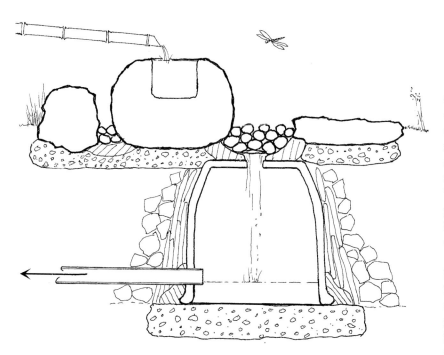

Suikinkutsu – the echo chamber that is sometimes placed below a water basin.

upside down on the base and completely sealed with waterproof mortar mix. The drainage system must then be connected to the lower hole of the pot and again sealed with waterproof mortar. Surround the pot with old tiles or slates to provide protection and then back-fill the hole with rubble. Care must be taken so that no earth or debris is washed down into the echo chamber, as this may gradually clog the

outlet. The surrounding rocks can put in place and a slightly dished fillet of waterproof mortar mix should then be applied to allow water to drain to the central drainage hole. The basin can then be positioned, and the cement can be covered up with some cobblestones.

Water can be brought to the basin through bamboo pipes, but these tend to split. To overcome this, knock out the nodal dividers inside the bamboo with a metal rod and insert some garden hosepipe. A regulating valve can be inserted into the hosepipe to control the flow of water into the basin. This is important, as the sound of the water falling into the basin is as significant as the amount of flow. If you do not want to waste water with a steady flow, fit a small recycling pump in a tank below the basin. Provision will need to be made for maintenance of the pump.

Water carried about the garden in split-bamboo pipes.

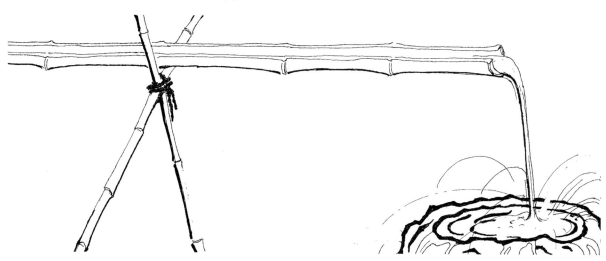

Shishi odoshi, or deer scarer, showing the striking stone and the filling pipe.

DEER SCARER

The 'deer scarer' or shishi odoshi has become popular with Western builders of Japanese gardens. Again, you should consider it simply as an artefact to be used in the garden design; it will not in itself make the garden any more Japanese.

A deer scarer is made from a bamboo pole that fills with water at one end and then over-balances, causing the pole to fall forward and the water to pour out. The pole then returns to a balanced position and loudly thwacks a strategically placed stone. If a feature emphasizing the passing of time is to be a necessary part of the garden's design, the rhythmical sound from a deer scarer can provide that element. However, that rhythmic sound could soon prove to be a constant irritation, and destroy the tranquillity that has been created.

Water to supply a deer scarer is usually recycled from a pond or stream, run along a system of hollowed or split-bamboo pipes.

A small pump is often sufficient to run this feature, as long as it has an adequate head height (see pages 77–8 for more information on pumps). Try to purchase a well-made unit that has a bound sounding pipe and has been properly waterproofed. Due to the constant splashing of water, splitting will undoubtedly occur in bamboo without adequate waterproofing, and the deer scarer will cease to function.

CHAPTER 6

Plants and Flowers

GENERAL PRINCIPLES

Plants are generally used in the Japanese garden in the same context as they would be found in nature. For example, if a mountainous landscape is being depicted, an iris would not be used. Similarly, a gardener aiming to achieve the effect of a sea coast would not plant a mountain maple like Acer palmatum. Even though the idea is to create an abstraction, the plants resonate in the viewer, and are surprisingly powerful in evoking memories of certain landscapes.

Incongruity of planting is a mistake often seen in the West when Japanese-style gardens are constructed. Some latitude is acceptable. For example, if an arrangement of a purely abstract style is being created, in an entrance space or courtyard, the textures of the plant life and the geometry of the design would assume greater importance than the actual species.

Much has been written and said about the necessity of using Japanese varieties of plants in a Japanese-style garden; this is mostly nonsense. The Japanese gardener uses the plants he finds around him, from his landscape and his culture. It is the way he interprets his culture and landscape through the plants that is exciting. The fundamentals of Japanese garden design are not about the type of plants used, but about the way those plants are used. Ask yourself why a gardener used this plant in this location, and why he put a particular plant next to it, and you will be led to select plants for your garden that have a similar habit and texture.

The Japanese gardener also uses certain plants because they have a seasonal or cultural association.

Opposite: *Giant wisteria, Karatsu Castle.*

Giant cycads, Hagi.

For example, pine is a symbol of longevity, while Ume, or wild apricot, represents fleeting beauty. These associations are usually understood when the plant is seen in its natural habit of, and in an exploration of the emotions that are stirred within the observer by the passing of time.

Climatic conditions will also dictate which plants may be used. The type of plant must suit the location of the garden. The climate in western Japan and Okinawa, for example, is ideal for cycads, podocarps, figs and palms, and many examples of these species are found in the gardens in those areas. A more 'honest' garden will be constructed if you take into consideration the landscape and climate of the place where you live. Your aim should not be slavishly to copy the surface features of the Japanese garden, but to create a garden that is Japanese in style and visually beautiful, using plant materials that are readily available and evocative of the landscape you are trying to suggest.

Some knowledge of the pH factor of the soil in the area you want to use will be helpful in choosing the

Red Ume.

Plant textures.

right plants for your garden. Simple soil-testing kits, inexpensive and readily available in garden centres, will assist you in identifying whether your soil is alkaline or acidic. Levels of acidity can change within the space of a few metres, so take readings from several points in the garden. A reading of 6.5 pH is neutral; above that, the level is alkaline and below, it is acidic.

Look at the variety of plants in your neighbours' gardens. They will be growing in soil conditions that are similar to yours, and the plants that are growing well there will usually grow well in your garden too. The plants available in your local nursery will probably also do well. The local nurseryman is unlikely to sell plants that he knows his customers will be bringing back after they have failed to survive.

Do not despair if you find that your soil is very alkaline, because alternative lime-tolerant plants can be used. However, if you desperately want to grow traditional acid-loving plants, you can try to achieve the effect you want through the use of raised beds or pots. Removing some of the offending soil and planting directly into the ground will not work, as the lime will eventually seep into the new compost,

Ancient moss garden, Ryoanji Temple, Kyoto.

causing the acid-loving plant to suffer from chlorosis and, eventually, to die. Lime can also be introduced, to the detriment of the plant, through watering; in hard-water areas, collected rainwater should be used for watering in the garden.

Before planting, all soils will benefit from the addition of garden compost or well-rotted manure. This will not only improve the soil's fertility but will also open up the texture of heavy clay soils and improve the water retention of light sandy soils.

It is your garden, so choose plants that will give you pleasure. Generally, try not to use too many types of plants in one area – two or three types will make a stronger statement – and consider how your design can bring them together in a traditional Japanese style.

GROUND-COVER PLANTS AND MOSSES

When choosing ground-cover plants to bring interest to a design, think about texture, colour and tone of colour, especially in small courtyard areas. The nearer the area is to your residence, the greater is its visual importance. Also, consider whether the soil conditions in the area are dry or moist and whether

the ground cover will be walked on, or not.

Moss is the epitome of ground cover in the Japanese garden, and there is no ideal substitute for the beautiful thick green carpet that it can produce. Some of the moss colonies in Japan are as ancient as the temples to which they belong, and may contain up to a hundred different varieties, giving an almost infinite number of shades of green. The work of tending the temples' moss gardens is looked upon as contemplative and devotional work; someone who toils to care for the temple may hope to gain eventual merit in heaven.

These moss gardens almost certainly developed because the gardens' microclimate was conducive to such growth. Once established, the moss was cared for and cultivated. The Japanese gardener has a love-hate relationship with moss; its power to cover the garden's rockwork completely is seen partly as an intrusion that buries and diminishes the beauty of the rocks. It also requires a significant amount of maintenance. On the other hand, moss is also beautiful and evokes feelings of timeless serenity.

There are about fifteen thousand varieties of moss, and each one has adapted to its own specific niche in the ecological system. They divide into two groups: one clings to the surface of the ground and creeps over it, and one has very simple embryonic roots, stalks and 'leaves'. Although there is a place for each in the Japanese garden, it is the second type that is used as ground cover. Another moss-like plant, Club moss, or Selaginella, is a useful rhizomatous perennial with creeping stems, which root as they grow along the ground, and have scale-like leaves. It grows in moss-like tufts, but it is frost-tender and likes high humidity.

If you find some nice thick attractive moss growing in woodland, and take it home to transplant into your garden, it will almost certainly die. This will not be because you have not cared for it properly, but because that variety may only grow in that particular place and will not be able to adapt to the conditions in your garden. However, if you know of a supply of moss that is growing in conditions similar to those you have, its chances of survival are greatly increased. The most favoured moss for Japanese-style gardens is the dark green Sugi or Cedar moss, so called because it is shaped like that tree; in Europe, it is generally referred to as Hair cap moss (*Polytrichum*).

If you want a moss garden, or just a small bed of healthy moss to bring attention to a special stone, the best way is to encourage the right mosses for your location to grow naturally. Whether you want to cover a small area or a large one, you need to prepare the ground, removing any existing grasses or weeds that might compete with or overshadow the moss.

Some lawns are already potentially moss gardens and large sums of money are spent each year on trying to kill the moss that continuously infiltrates them. It seems to be impossible to find a herbicide that will kill all the grass and leave all of the moss. However, they do not usually have an effect on moss, so it is quite acceptable to prepare the ground by using weedkillers to deal with unwanted grasses and plants. The main advantage that moss has over grass as ground cover is that you do not have to mow it.

Moss tends to grow where there is shade and moisture, in sticky compacted soil, with good drainage below. It particularly likes clay and sandy soils, which are acidic. After weeding and clearing the area, roll it, rake it and keep it moist. The acidity of the soil can be increased with the sprinkling of a proprietary soil acidifier or rhododendron fertilizer – 5.5 pH is ideal. Then you have to wait…and wait; it may take several years before you get the results that you want. If moss is already growing in your garden, try collecting some, drying it, crumbling it up and sprinkling it where you have prepared the soil. This will spread the spores and encourage further growth.

Remember that it is illegal to collect mosses from many publicly accessible areas such as Forestry Commission land, where a licence is required. If friends have areas or ditches where moss that is suitable for your garden grows freely, take advantage of it. Do not just lift the green part of the moss, but lift all of its roots and the soil in which it is growing. Close-plant the moss edge to edge in the same way that you would plant any other shallow-rooted plants. Collecting sufficient moss to cover a large area may be difficult so, in this case, plant the mosses in equidistant clumps. With good care and regular watering, the gaps should soon fill in. Plant the clumps firmly or, if they are particularly small, anchor them into the ground with pieces of bent wire so that they are more resistant to the tugging of inquisitive blackbirds. Watering, on at least a daily basis, will be vital for the first couple of years. After that, watering

Grass as a ground cover.

should only be necessary during dry spells to ensure that the moss does not dry out completely.

Being moisture-loving, mosses tend to grow better during the wetter winter months, and denying them sunlight during the first summer may help them to develop. Rocaleen or similar shade netting with about 40 per cent shade factor may help in providing the right conditions. The drier, browned texture of the moss during the summer months does not meant that is dead; often, the moss is restored to its full glory with the return of wet weather. Remember, though, that there are no guarantees, as moss requires a very specific microclimate. If it does not want to grow, you cannot make it do so. If it chooses not to grow in your garden, go for a substitute.

If the area in question is large enough, ordinary lawn grass can be used to give cover but you must be able to cut the grass effectively around rocks and over any undulations. A plant often used now is Tamaryu or Rynohige, known as Dwarf snake's beard or Lilyturf, which is a dwarf green form of Ophiopogon. It is extremely tolerant of shade and is fully hardy. Kumasasa, the dwarf bamboo Sasa, is also fully hardy, but tends to wither at the margins in the winter and is extremely invasive (see pages 99–101, for more on bamboo).

Low ground cover can be achieved with plants such as Dwarf thyme (*Thymus*) or Pearlwort (*Sagina*). The majority of pearlworts are treated as weeds but there are several cultivated varieties that have dense mats or cushions of leaves. The dwarf thymes not only give good ground cover' but are also lime-tolerant and release a pleasant fragrance when they are walked on. Decorative ferns are often recommended for use in Japanese gardens but most ferns are frost-tender and die back in the winter, so they only give a really good ground cover in the summer months. They can be put to better use as decorative accents beside a rock or at the base of a wall.

Cotoneaster as a ground cover.

One under-used ground-cover plant is the small decorative ivy (*Hedera*), which is usually sold in garden centres as a houseplant. There are many useful varieties that are generally very hardy and perfectly able to survive the coldest of winters. If left to grow along the ground, it can quickly cover an area, and has the added advantage of being able to grow even in dry shade. When ivies get older their leaves lose their lobed appearance and become ovate, so it may be necessary to prune them back on a regular basis to encourage their juvenile growth.

Many of the alpine plants that make cushions go well in conjunction with moss and lichen-encrusted rocks in areas that need detail. Saxifrages can be particularly useful as the different types vary greatly in habit, leaf form and colouring. They are hardy, most are evergreen and they are not as susceptible to winter dampness as some other alpine plants. As a bonus, they flower and are tolerant of most soil conditions.

Pachysandra, Fukkiso, makes a good evergreen ground-cover shrub that grows to about 20cm high and has leaves about 5cm long. Sweet box (*Sarcococca*) makes good cover for woodland settings and Common box is available in dwarfed varieties such as *Buxus microphylla var.* and *B. insularis var.*, which will make interesting ground cover when clipped and kept low. Many of the low-growing evergreen cotoneasters are also useful. I have used several varieties of cotoneaster to produce gently undulating beds of ground cover, clipping them twice a year to neaten the shape. Ardisia (Maniryo), the marlberry, is another useful evergreen shrub that is hardy to about minus 5 degrees centigrade and shade-tolerant. It has a natural low-growing habit and will not need much regular pruning. As a bonus, Cotoneaster, Ardisia and Sarcococca types bear red or black berries in the winter. They all like damp, humus-rich soil, but are also fairly tolerant of dry spells and neglect. If your soil is relatively uniformly acidic throughout the planting area, you could also consider the dwarf varieties of rhododendron.

Prostrate forms of Parahebe make dense mats of leathery leaves that are extremely effective when seen tumbling over walls or large rocks. It likes dry, sunny conditions and can tolerate very poor soil conditions. Often, it will grow in a position where some of the more usual ground-cover plants will not thrive sufficiently well to give the effect that you want to create.

BAMBOO

In Oriental cultures, bamboo is more than an attractive garden plant – it is essential in sustaining both body and soul. Providing aesthetic materials for the arts, food from its shoots, and building materials from its adult canes, it is intrinsic to the Oriental way of life. It is, therefore, very tempting to want to include this plant in a Japanese garden.

There are many different bamboo species to chose from that like to grow in moist conditions in humus-rich soil, tolerating both full sun or partial shade. The Phyllostachys var. species are the most dramatic, ranging from the tall and ethereal to the kinked and knobbly. They grow in numerous shades of green and yellow, and in black, and are excellent for courtyard garden features. The clump-forming Arundinaria species are less vigorous than some of the other varieties and are quite good for rustic screening devices.

The bamboo stalk is known as the 'culm', and only referred to as a cane when it has been dried. When it first shoots, the culm is already at its maximum width and contains all of the nodes it will have when it reaches its full height. Its rapid growth simply extends the distance between these nodes.

If bamboo is to be used as a feature in your garden, it should be started from a rhizome that has running roots that constantly regenerate. Several rhizomes

Bamboo in the snow.

a planting depth of 15–25cm. Remember that this is the depth of water above the plant, and does not include the depth of the crate in which the lily has been planted.

Most water-lilies have thick tuber-like rhizomes that grow horizontally with their roots below them. Trim back any old or damaged leaves, leaving only new short leaves or buds, as old leaves make the plant buoyant and difficult to stabilize. Planting should follow the general rules and only be done when the water had lost its winter chill, using a rich loam to which special water-lily fertilizer can be added if desired.

Lilies' roots need checking regularly as they can quickly outgrow their basket and spread across the bottom of the pond, leaving little room for other plants to grow, and for fish to manoeuvre. When trimming or dividing water-lilies it may be useful to wear rubber gloves as the tubers can stain skin brown.

Although they are the most popular, water-lilies are not the only deep-water plants with floating leaves. The Water hawthorn Aponogeton distachyos has double spikes of fragrant white flowers, with contrasting black anthers, that are held just above the water. It has strap-like floating leaves and is more tolerant of cold than water-lilies are. It flowers in the spring and in the autumn, and should be planted at a depth of between 25 and 75cm.

Water violets and Water crowfoot are useful and also flower above the water, but have most of their leaves submerged (see below for more on submerged plants).

Submerged Plants

If there is no filtration system in the pond, oxygenating plants, usually referred to as water weeds, are vital if the water is not to stagnate. All plants release oxygen but, as the leaves of water weeds are totally submerged, they release oxygen directly into the water.

Whatever oxygenator you choose, a minimum of five bunches will be needed for each square metre of surface area. Loam is not really needed as a planting material in most cases, as the roots of water weeds are there for anchorage rather than for gaining nutrients, and pea shingle or gravel will usually suffice. If submerged plants that flower above the surface are used, these should be planted up using a heavy loam in the same manner as marginal plants.

Opposite: *Water hawthorn in a slow-flowing stream.*

The best known of the water weeds is the Canadian pondweed *Elodea canadensis*, and *E. crispa*, both of which will easily root into the mud at the bottom of the pond and should be planted in small weighted bunches. The soft shoots are, however, very attractive to Koi carp and are sometimes quickly eaten. Any small bits that break off will easily root and, although the weed you put in a new pond never looks as thought it is sufficient, new ponds are so rich in nutrients that the weed will grow very quickly into a dense mat.

Starwort, *Callitriche bermaphroditica*, is a very useful oxygenator as it is active in the winter as well as the summer. It grows in a tight mass of light green leaves that grow in stiff whirls on slender stems. The milfoils *Myriophyllum* are also good oxygenators and have bright green needle-like leaves. The soft stems of Parrot's feather milfoil can often be seen protruding from shallow water and will creep over the edges of the pond.

Hornwort, *Ceratophyllum demersum*, is completely adapted to aquatic life as it flowers and pollinates under water. It does not have any roots and will either use small rhizoids to anchor itself in the mud or will float freely. Hornwort is the only water weed that genuinely does not need planting, and only needs to be 'thrown' into the pond. It will find its own level and each small piece will grow into an erect plant with attractive, curly, coarse leaves. The coarseness of its leaves discourages fish from eating them, making it ideal as a pond oxygenator.

Water violets *Hottonia palustris* and Water crowfoots *Ranunculus aquatilis* are good oxygenators with submerged leaves, and, as they both flower above water, they can serve a dual purpose.

It is difficult to advise which of these is the best water weed, as the best weed for your pond is the one that grows and flourishes better than any of the others. Try planting several to see which one grows best in your pond. Once it is established, you will be removing it by the barrow-load several times a year (see pages 134–5 for more on maintenance).

MOISTURE-LOVING PLANTS FOR BOGGY AREAS

As a group, the moisture-loving plants are very valuable in the Japanese garden from the design point of view. To get the best effect, consider texture, shape

and leaf colour when selecting your plant combinations. There are many large-leafed and round-leafed architectural varieties that can be contrasted with the sword-like leaves of irises and the tall flower spikes of other boggy plants. The general principle of a bold statement rather than a mass planting is just as relevant to the bog plants as it is to any other aspect of the Japanese garden.

There are no set rules about which plants you should use; it is your garden and your favourite plants should be there. The following list of plants is intended only as a guide. The ranges stocked by local garden centres are now fairly extensive but some of the less common varieties may need to be ordered from a specialist supplier.

Hosta

Plants of the Hosta family, the Plantain lilies, vary in height and leaf size, from large to miniature, and in colour, from butter yellow to blueish-green. New cultivars appear at flower shows every year, and the range of colour combination and size is constantly being extended.

Although hostas are grown mainly for their foliage, they do flower in midsummer, producing spikes of white, mauve or violet flowers above their foliage. *Hosta sieboldiana* is the largest and most vigorous of the Hosta family and can grow to a height of 60cm, with an eventual spread of 1.5m. They like moist soil that is fairly well drained, and benefit from a rich mulch in the spring. Hostas prefer full sun or partial shade; they will tolerate full shade, but it will severely reduce their flowering.

When planting hostas, ensure that the smaller varieties are not totally overwhelmed by their larger-leafed neighbours. While the majority of perennials are planted with their crown at soil level, hostas prefer to be shallow-planted, with their crowns about 2cm below ground surface.

Ligularia

Varieties of the large-leafed Ligularia family will enhance any Japanese-style garden and are now fairly easy to find in garden centres. *L. dentata* grows

Opposite: *Equisetum hymale, or Horsetail.*

up to 1-1.5m in height, has large round leathery leaves and produces orange daisy flowers in midsummer. *L. dentata* 'Desdemona' is more compact and has deep red leaves that are even darker underneath, while *L. dentata* 'Gregynog Gold' has round leaves of deep green. *L. stenocephala* is tall, has triangular, jagged-tooth, green foliage and is fast-growing. *L. przewalskii* is a spectacular plant with attractive black stems, large, light green, deeply cut leaves and tall, long-lasting spikes of small golden flowers. It likes a rich damp soil and can reach a height of nearly 2m.

Rheum and Rodgersia

Ornamental rhubarb of the Rheum family grows in a range of habitats but prefers a moist, humus-rich soil. As with the Ligularia family, Rheum leaves come in shades of green and in red. This, with the variation in leaf size and shape, adds even more interest to the plant group. The Rodgersia family likes the same conditions and has large, long-stalked, green leaves. Both Rheum and Rodgersia flower, but are usually grown for their foliage interest.

Crambe and Gunnera

Although it is not truly a bog plant, Crambe cordifolia has long-stalked, kidney-shaped, dark green leaves that grow up to 35cm across and is useful if a large-leafed plant is needed. It has masses of tiny white star-shaped flowers borne on many-branched panicles in late spring and midsummer, and grows to a height of 1.5m. If you are looking for a very large plant, Gunnera produces huge leaves in the right conditions. However, Gunnera can be temperamental, as it needs permanently moist ground and will require winter frost protection; this can be achieved by laying straw, or its dead leaves, over the crown.

Iris

Iris kaempferi (*I. ensata*) likes damp acid soil but does not like it to be waterlogged. It grows to a height of 60-80cm and its sword-like leaves have a very distinct mid rib. This iris is rather exotic and comes in many beautiful shades. The less showy varieties are most commonly sought for the Japanese garden. *I. sibirica* has more slender leaves than most irises and is happy in moist ground; its flowers are as beautiful as those of *I. kaempferi* and have distinct yellow or white veining in the petals.

Ferns

Ferns are always effective and range widely in frond size, shape and texture in those varieties that favour moist soil. Of the more delicate ferns, the Adiantum and Asplenium are the most attractive, but many of the cultivars are far too tender for growing in the garden. However, *Adiantum pedatum*, or Maidenhair fern, and *Adiantum venustum* will grow well in sheltered places. Both have lovely pale green drooping fronds with black stems.

Asplenium trichomanes, or Maidenhair spleenwort, resembles the Adiantum with its light green leaves and black stems, but it likes lime-rich soil. *Asplenium scolopendrium*, the Hart's-tongue fern, has leaves that are bright green, smooth and leathery. Many Hart's-tongue fern cultivars have leaves that become frillier and frillier.

Of the larger ferns, the Buckler fern Dryopteris is hardy, but deciduous, and grows to 1m in height. *Athyrium filix-femina*, or Lady fern, is of similar height, will tolerate a variety of conditions except drought, and has lovely delicate fronds. Japanese painted fern *Athyrium nipponicum* is shorter and has silvery grey-green fronds with red-purple mid ribs. There are also many useful attractive ferns in the

Stone wall with ferns, Nara, Japan.

Polystichum group. If height is required, *Osmunda regalis*, or Royal fern, will grow up to 2m high.

Horsetails

The horsetails of the Equisetum family are useful as a vertical element in the design of the Japanese garden, but can be very invasive. They look particularly good around the water basin and lantern arrangement, as they complement the upright form of the lantern. There are many varieties, from low-growing clump forms to *E. hymale*, which reaches a height of 1m.

Peonies

Peonies (of the Paeonia family) are technically neither Japanese plants nor bog plants but they do fit well into the Japanese-style garden, with large saucer- or cup-shaped flowers framed by bold dissected leaves. If left alone, peonies will flourish for many years, but they do resent disturbance and it can be several years before a plant will flower again if it has been moved. They are generally fully hardy and like a rich moist soil, which should not be too deep over the crown. Often, when mulches and fertilizers are heaped on the plant, it will refuse to flower; in order to avoid this, put any added compost around the plant rather than on top of it.

Lilies

It is hard to imagine the serenity of a Japanese garden without also thinking of the beauty and elegance of lilies. Many books have been devoted to the wide subject of lily growing, so below are details of only those varieties that will give the desired result for your purposes, and are easy to grow in a European climate.

Plant lilies in the autumn in soil that is moist but well drained, and enriched with leaf mould or organic compost. Most lilies prefer acid conditions but some are lime-tolerant. The bulbs should be plump and firm and should be planted at a depth of at least three times the bulb's height. This is especially important in those species that are stem-rooting. The majority of lilies like to be planted with their base in the shade and their flowers in full sun: a few are shade tolerant but none like to be planted in deep shade.

Lilium auratum is a spectacular Japanese species known as the Golden-rayed lily because of its wide saucer-shaped white flowers. It is tall, growing between 90cm and 1.5m in height and bearing ten or more intensely fragrant flowers per stem. It is fairly tolerant of soil conditions but flourishes best in lime-free soil. *L. speciosum* is another fragrant Japanese lily that flowers later in the year, often into the autumn. The flowers are long, pendant and have petals that are rolled back like a Turk's cap. *Var. album* is white and *var. rubrum* is dark pink; several other colour variations may be found.

Most Oriental hybrid lilies have been developed from *L. auratum* and *L. speciosum* and from the Chinese species *L. henryi*; all of them are spectacularly beautiful with a memorable fragrance. 'Casa Blanca' has enormous, almost flat, white flowers with brown stamens, while 'Star Gazer' is crimson in colour. 'Imperial Gold' has large, fragrant, star-shaped, glistening white flowers with a yellow stripe down the centre of each petal.

L. henryi is one of the easiest to grow of all the lilies. It is exceptionally tall (2m), with broad leaves that get smaller towards the top of the plant. It has bright orange Turk's cap flowers that are spotted darker towards the centre, and is useful, as it will grow in semi-shade and tolerates alkaline soil.

L. candidum, the Madonna lily, needs a warm, sunny position. It is actually a Mediterranean plant, but can be used effectively in a Japanese-style garden as its flowers are superb, numerous and fragrant. It is also tall, growing to a height of about 1.5m.

The Regal lily *L. regale* is another that is easy to grow. It is hardy, tolerates a wide range of soil conditions, and flowers from seed in just three years. The flowers are fragrant and up to 15cm long in either plain white (album) or with a purple staining on the outside (rubrum).

New varieties are being developed all the time and there have been major developments in the shorter dwarf varieties in recent years. When choosing your lily, think about the overall composition of the planting, selecting the size and colour to give the effect you desire. The lilies' magnificent fragrance will bring an added dimension to your overall scheme.

CLIMBING PLANTS

Wisteria is a woody, twining, deciduous plant that will give a dramatic finish to any wall or garden structure, and can even be trained as a half-standard tree. The Japanese variety *Wisteria floribunda* has extremely long white, blue or pinkish racemes that can grow up to 1m in length, and have been known to reach 2m in one cultivar. The pea-like flowers are fragrant, and open gradually from the top to the bottom. *W. sinensis*, the Chinese wisteria, is more rampant and has smaller leaves and shorter racemes than its Japanese cousin. The flowers on the racemes of the Chinese variety open all at the same time. It has also been noted that the Japanese variety twines in a clockwise direction while the Chinese wisteria twines in an anti-clockwise direction.

It may take several years for a young wisteria plant to flower, and it will need pruning twice a year if it is to flower properly, but it is worth the effort. Wisterias prefer to grow in rich, moist, but well-drained soil in partial shade or full sun, and will generally need some kind of support unless growing through a pergola or tree.

The clematis is not a Japanese plant but is still very useful in the Japanese-style garden, as it offers such a wide range of flower colour, size and shape. Like the lilies, there are so many different varieties of clematis that many books have been devoted exclusively to the species. Clematis has both early and late flowering varieties, so it is possible to extend the flowering season by planting different sorts. Remember the general principles of Japanese gardening and avoid those that are overly flamboyant.

Clematis prefer rich, moist soil and will benefit from a winter mulch of well-rotted compost. All varieties should be planted with the crown at least 8cm below soil level in order to avoid shoot damage and clematis wilt. Although clematis likes its head in the sun, the roots should be kept cool and this can be accomplished by allowing the roots to spread beneath a rock or paving stone. As with wisteria, support will be needed for this plant unless it is growing through a tree.

Jasmine is also an attractive and fragrant flowering climber, as is the climbing hydrangea. For autumn colour, the Virginia creeper *Parthenocissus* is hard to beat. Truly rampant climbers such as the Russian vine *Polygonaceae* should be avoided at all costs.

Opposite: *Wisteria.*

CHAPTER 7

Trees and Shrubs

TREES

General Principles

When considering trees for a Japanese-style garden, pines and maples automatically come to mind, but a wide variety of evergreen and deciduous trees can be used. Siting a tree is a major design decision and its ultimate height, spread and growth rate are very important. Although trees are valued mainly for the architectural qualities, they can also provide interest through their flowers, berries and bark.

Opposite: *Japanese red pine, Jokuriji Temple.*

The main types of pine used in Japanese gardens are Japanese white pine *Pinus pentaphyla* and Japanese red pine *P. densiflora*. The Scots pine *P. sylvestris* looks very much like red pine and is easily found in nurseries and garden centres. It will require proper pruning and training though, as styling of nursery stock is virtually unknown in the West; fortunately, it responds very readily to training techniques. Many of the dwarf cultivars of pines may also be useful, as they already resemble small trees of a reasonable shape. Cultivars to look out for are *P. sylvestris* 'Beuvronensis' or 'Doone Valley', and the dwarf cultivars of *P. densiflora* such as

Red maple.

'Umbraculifera'. Dwarf cultivars of other pines can be used if they are not too showy. However, remember that even these would be trained in Japan, and that you will have to train your trees if they are to look as though they 'belong' in a Japanese-style garden. Japanese black pine *P. thunbergii* is also used in Japanese-style gardens, but not as readily as other varieties. However, it is very useful in coastal situations.

Several of the deciduous trees suitable for the Japanese-style garden are flowering, such as Japanese flowering apricot, Ume (*Prunus mume*), and flowering cherry, Sakura (*Prunus spp.*). They are planted to reflect the changing seasons. *Cercis siliquastrum*, the Judas tree, and *Cercidiphyllum japonicum*, the Katsura tree, are good for spring interest as are the Crab-apple trees *Malus spp.*, all of which have a compact habit. Deciduous trees are bare of their leaves for six months of the year so, if year-round interest is to be maintained, their appearance when leafless is important in the garden's design. Many deciduous trees are considered by the Japanese to be at their best in the winter months when their branch structure is evident.

The mountain maple *Acer palmatum* is the tree most people would associate with the Japanese garden, usually through the cut-leafed cultivars of the 'Dissectum' group. The palmatum species is incredible for its ability to sport hundreds of varieties producing many interesting leaf colours and sizes. Unfortunately, the leaves of many of these cultivars are delicate and become badly damaged by late frosts and coastal winds. Great care is needed when buying and choosing a site for these maples.

The true green form of *A. palmatum* is a beautiful tree and should be far more widely available than it is. A mountain tree, it tends to be much stronger and more vigorous than the fancy cultivars, many of which are overpriced because they are grafted on to this ordinary stock. Again, these cultivars should be

Opposite: *Pink Ume.*

White cherry.

planted with restraint, as many are too showy. Remember that the fine tracery of winter twigs is greatly appreciated in Japan.

Other maples that should be considered are the Full-moon maple *A. japonicum*; its 'Aureum' variety, the Golden full-moon maple; the Trident maple *A. buergeranum*, and the Amur maple *A. ginnala*, both of which have fabulous autumn colour. The Snake-bark maples *A. rufinerve* are very showy and their habit tends to be rather coarse, so they are best avoided, except in a larger garden.

Many of the Oriental hornbeams are quite delicate in habit and are worth growing. They are attractive for their autumn colour, which is mainly yellow to red, unlike the European hornbeam, which turns a rather dowdy brown. Mountain ashes or rowans (*Sorbus*) are mostly quite small trees with a delicate

Styled trees.

Opposite: *Maples in Kyoto.*

habit, and autumn leaf and berry interest that makes them suitable for the Japanese garden. Birch (*Betula*) is not common in Japanese gardens, even though many varieties give a pleasing delicate foliage effect (see page 66, on lighting). The white ones are considered too showy and birches, generally, are short-lived.

Camellias, or Susanqua, are seen covering entire hillsides in Japan and are often used in gardens as feature plants to reflect the season. In areas that are prone to snow and frosts, their emerging blossoms are sometimes protected from the burning effects of extreme cold by funny straw hats. Camellias are in the same family as Stewartia, the tea family, which also have good autumn colour and lovely, smooth, cinnamon-coloured bark.

Small-leafed holly, *Ilex crenata*, is grown in Japan as a tall clipped tree or in the form of a clipped bush. Any imported stock should be carefully checked for disease, as this has been a problem with some trees in recent years. Enkianthus is also usually found in shrub form but can grow into a small tree with good seasonal colour.

Western red cedar (*Thuja plicata*) is sometimes recommended, but be wary of trees that grow so tall. They can reach a height of 30m, with a trunk diameter of 3-4m, and can become hollow inside, necessitating drastic measures for their removal. Hinoki cypress *Chamaecyparis obtusa* and Sugi, *Cryptomeria japonica*, can both be used, but they also grow to a large size, so careful siting is necessary. Both are also found in a range of dwarfed cultivars, which can be useful if they are not too showy.

Larch, or *Larix*, can be quickly trained to produce a 'garden-style' tree but is not often seen in Japanese gardens because it is not tolerant of the hot summers experienced in Tokyo and Kyoto. This is less of a problem in northern Europe but, as the tree drops millions of yellow needles in autumn, it can make maintenance of the garden difficult.

Junipers are very useful in the Japanese garden, both as ground cover and as specimen shrubs, as they are slow growing. The Temple juniper *Juniperus rigida* is a mountain tree and can be difficult to cultivate in some garden conditions as it requires a high level of moisture. Some of the semi-prostrate varieties, such as *J. chinensis* 'San José', are accustomed to more arid conditions and can be clipped to shape to suggest clouds around rock groupings, for example. The truly prostrate varieties, such as *J. procumbens* or *J. horizontalis*, form a thick carpet and make good ground cover.

The wide range of foliage tone and colour, from yellow green through to silvery and blue shades, can be used to relate plant colour to specific rock groupings or to contrast with other foliage plants.

One of the first trees to colour in the autumn, giving spectacular shades of red, is *Rhus verniciflua*, the Varnish or Lacquer tree. It makes a useful specimen tree but care needs to be taken when choosing this tree, as it throws out runners that travel a long way from the parent tree. Also, the tree has a tendency to be fairly short-lived and has sap that can

Rock with junipers.

cause quite intense allergic reactions in some people.

Of the deciduous flowering trees, magnolias must be the most dramatic. The magnolia's Japanese name is Kobushi, which means 'fist', describing the shape of its flower buds. Care must also be taken when choosing varieties of this tree as some can take many years to flower and others have a tendency to grow large and require considerable pruning. The Star magnolia *Magnolia stellata*, which grows wild in Japan is smaller and more delicate in appearance than the larger *M. soulangeana*, but both are lovely trees to have in the garden, especially as they flower early in the spring before their leaves appear. *M. stellata*, which also has a delicate pink variety, has an additional benefit as its flowers are less likely to suffer from wind and frost damage than those of some other varieties.

Selecting and Planting Trees

Trees can be bought as pot-grown, rootballed or bare-rooted. Although conifers are seldom seen as bare-rooted specimens, deciduous trees are often sold in this form. Only buy bare-rooted trees when they are dormant, as they will almost certainly die if they are transplanted when in leaf. The best time for purchase is in the autumn or early spring. Check that the tree has a good root spread and avoid those trees that have roots only on one side, as they will also have problems in becoming established.

Rootballed trees have been grown in the open ground and lifted with the soil around their roots intact to protect the root from too much damage and disturbance. The rootball is then wrapped in hessian or plastic mesh to stop the soil falling off and the roots drying out. Larger specimens of conifers or deciduous trees are often sold in this way. These trees should have been undercut every two to three years to encourage inner root growth so the tree has the maximum chance of survival when it is lifted. Unfortunately, this is seldom done and often the soil falls away to reveal almost no roots.

Bare-root and rootballed trees are lifted after the first frost and they should be planted immediately after collection to avoid frost damage. Autumn-planted trees have a much better chance of surviving dry spells in the spring or summer than those that have been planted in midwinter or early spring. Before planting, it is essential that bare-root trees have their roots thoroughly soaked in water for several hours.

Container-grown trees can be planted at any time of the year and usually survive more successfully than bare-root or rootballed specimens as there is minimal root disturbance. However, they are usually more expensive than bare-root or rootballed trees of a comparable size.

Before buying a container-grown tree, try to inspect its roots, if you can, by removing it from the pot. See that the root is healthy and not pot-bound. Pot-bound trees, or those with thick roots protruding from the bottom of the pot, do not establish themselves well and should be avoided. If the soil falls away from the roots, it shows that the root system is not well developed, and this can also lead to problems, as the trees may be unstable when planted.

Some bare-root or rootballed trees are potted at the end of the season and sold as containerized plants for higher prices, so beware.

When deciding which tree to buy in a nursery, choose one that looks vigorous and has an even distribution of roots and branches. It is often better to buy a smaller good-looking healthy tree than to go for the biggest. Sometimes, however, when I am looking for trees for a Japanese-style garden, I often buy misshapen neglected stock, as it may be more interesting from a design point of view. You need a good understanding of how to bring the vigour back into the tree if you buy in this way. However, interesting shape can be cut into an ordinary tree as will be seen in the section on pruning.

Most trees need a soil depth of about one metre if they are to flourish. Some will survive in shallower depths, but they are usually unstable and have difficulty coping with drought conditions. Pines like a well-drained soil in full sun, maples prefer more moist conditions with plenty of humus and are tolerant of some shade. The place where you plant your tree will already have been decided in your overall plan.

When planting your tree, you will need to dig a hole about three times the diameter of the rootball, and about one and half times its depth. Put the removed soil on a plastic sheet and mix it with compost, organic material, or a little bonemeal. Scarify the sides of the hole to loosen the soil and back-fill the hole to the required depth with the soil/compost mixture. All newly planted trees should be staked. The time to do this is before the tree is planted so that there is no damage to the tree's roots. Use either three guy wires firmly staked into the ground, or two good stakes with a brace between, and connect the tree to this arrangement with some cushioning, such as old rubber inner tubes, to protect the bark.

Fill the hole with water and allow it to soak away. Place the tree in the hole and spread the roots out evenly. If your tree is container-grown, and the roots have started to wind their way around the sides of the pot, tease a few of the roots away from the rootball, otherwise those roots will continue to grow in a spiral rather than spreading out into the surrounding soil. Make sure the tree is at the required depth and refill the hole with the soil/compost mixture. Firm the area thoroughly with your foot, and water well. You will need to water the tree during dry spells until it has established a good root system, which usually takes about two years.

Styled Trees

Trees already styled for Japanese gardens are becoming more frequently available in the West, but the number of species allowed for importation is limited both by the Ministry of Agriculture and by European Union regulations.

The only pine available from Japan that meets current EU health regulations is the Japanese white pine *Pinus parviflora*. These imported white pines are available in a variety of stages of development The older and more developed the tree, the better it is suited for its purpose, and the more highly priced. You can expect to pay from £8,000 to £10,000 for a large mature white pine. Large Japanese yews are also available from £5,000 to £8,000 per tree, while the small-leafed Japanese holly tends to be a bit less expensive. A few other varieties, such as Japanese maple and *Enkianthus*, can also be found in various stages of development. Styled trees will require careful maintenance and it is essential that you learn how to care for them properly as losses will be very expensive.

Styled Japanese yew.

Opposite: *Styled pines.*

If you have time to allow your garden to mature naturally, smaller trees can be purchased and developed further. Alternatively, you can grow and style your own trees, but this is a very long process.

Styling Your Own Trees

Good mature trees and bushes can often be found in neglected gardens and, if collected properly, will instantly add much 'character' to the garden. If you have existing trees it may be possible to prune these to a suitable style (see pages 128–9, for information on pruning trees).

Another source of characterful material for Japanese gardens is old neglected stock from garden centres and nurseries, where trees with sinuous

Trained pine, Kiyomizu Temple.

Opposite: *Clipped tree.*

interesting trunks can sometimes be found. Often, with a bit of encouragement, these plants can be brought back to health and vigour and the interesting lines that have been caused by die-back and neglect can be developed to fit your design.

When attempting to style a nursery tree yourself, consult Bonsai instruction manuals for help on deciding which branches to keep and which to remove. For older trees, look at photographs and drawings of Japanese gardens and see how minimalist some of them are. Do not remove branches in haste; allow time for your garden to develop. You can always remove another branch, but you cannot put it back on.

CLIPPED BUSHES

In the Japanese garden, clipped plants are used to represent rocks or clouds, geometric shapes or abstract forms. The idea of using bushes to represent rocks is thought to have arisen when the price and availability of good rocks restricted their general use. Allowing a clipped bush to take the place of a rock lightens the visual 'weight' of that element of the design, at the same time retaining the compositional structure. It also brings a slightly different texture to the composition, and harmonizes well with the rest of the 'green' in the garden. Clipped bushes proved to be a successful innovation for the Japanese gardener.

The most frequently used varieties of shrub for clipping are the Japanese azalea Satsuki, *Rhododendron indicum,* or the Japanese evergreen *Azalea kurume,* which is more common in Europe. Japanese small-leafed holly *Ilex crenata* and *Enkianthus campanulatus* are also very popular. Large plants of Japanese azalea and Japanese holly are difficult to acquire in Europe. There are imports from Japan but the price is, of course, very high.

Common box *Buxus sempervirens* works very well as a substitute when clipped to shape, as it has a leaf size and texture similar to Japanese holly. Large plants of many of the box family are readily available and most varieties grow quite quickly.

Some varieties of *Peris japonica* can also be used and large plants are quite often available; avoid the large-leafed ones such as 'Forest Flame', and go for compact varieties such as 'Saraband'. Yew (*Taxus*) is

Clipped box in a private garden.

Opposite: *Clipped bushes.*

also a possibility, but the texture and colour are quite different. Privet might also provide a good substitute.

Depending on their size, the plants will need to be planted 20cm apart in a diamond-shaped pattern. Box plants are best planted in the required site and then thickly mulched with partly rotted spent mushroom compost. This will help retain moisture in the soil for the first year, and nourish the plants as they grow. Mushroom compost has quite a lot of lime in it, which is fine for box, but should never be used for mulching azaleas or other lime-intolerant plants. Composted fine-grade bark is better for acid-loving plants.

Common box will eventually become a small tree if left to grow unchecked, and there is no problem with leaving it to grow tall if you require larger bushes. Box is also available in dwarfed varieties such as *Buxus microphylla var.* and *insularis var.*, which will make interesting ground covers, and can be clipped and kept low (see pages 95–9 for more on ground cover).

If they are to be controlled, the bushes will have to be clipped regularly. Azaleas should be clipped soon after flowering, when the new growth has hardened. If flowering plants are pruned too late in the year, the flower buds are pruned away with the wood and flowering for next year is greatly reduced. Box can be clipped when the new growth has hardened in June, and then given a final clip if necessary in the first week of September. This gives time for the cuts to heal before the frosts arrive.

Other Shrubs

While many of the bushes and shrubs to be found in the Japanese garden will have been clipped or styled, others are planted for their sumptuous leaves or flowers.

The Common hydrangea, *Hydrangea macrophylla*, grows wild in the coastal areas of Japan and is hardy in Europe. Before the introduction of sugar, the leaves of one variety were used to make Amancha, the sweet tea that was drunk on Buddha's birthday. There are two groups of *H. macrophylla*: lacecaps have flattened flower heads with small fertile flowers in the centre, and mopheads have spherical flower heads. Colouring of the flowers often depends on the level of acidity of the soil in which the plants grow. Acid soil leads to blue flowers whereas the more alkaline soils produce pink flowers; white-flowered varieties are not generally affected by the pH factor. They can grow to a height of 2m and prefer a moist, well-drained, humus-rich soil in sun or partial shade.

The Japanese fatsia, the False caster oil plant, or *Fatsia japonica*, is an evergreen plant that is often used in courtyard gardens. It has large, deep-lobed leathery leaves of 30cm or more and has small creamy white flowers in autumn. It can grow to between 1.5 and 4m tall and is tolerant of shade and city pollution, making it ideal for adding architectural interest to many of the Japanese garden forms. Fatshedera is of the same genus as Fatsia (*Araliacae*), but is much smaller in leaf size and in height.

CHAPTER 8

Maintenance

GENERAL PRINCIPLES

The maintenance of a garden is the last phase in its biography. The first phase was the need or vision leading to the creation of a garden. The inspiration for the design of the garden followed and then a commitment was made to actually build it. The detailed planning of how it should be carried out evolved into the hard practical work of realizing the initial goal or dream. At a certain point, the work seemed to be complete and the results could be observed and the building process reflected upon. However, that is not the end of the story – a garden does not stand still, but constantly evolves. Here is another lesson to be learned – the acceptance of responsibility for our actions.

An attention to order and cleanliness is a fundamental tenet of the Buddhist religion and its practice is crucial to understanding the true meanings of the Japanese garden. The constant maintenance of the garden is just as essential to its development as the building of it. Through maintenance, the garden develops its character and remains a healthy environment in which plants can grow.

Over the seasons and years, a garden changes and the clear plan that was designed is gradually eroded and eventually disappears under the needs of nature. The garden will be lost without a periodic injection of energy and a renewal of the vision from which the garden grew. This is not a case of slavery to a plan, but is an opportunity to improve the shaping, restore the

Opposite: *Cleaning the moss garden.*

Branch protection, Kanazawa, Japan.

vigour and watch the design unfold itself in an exciting way.

Each time work is done on the garden, it changes in ways that could never have been visualized initially. The garden will start to have a character and life of its own. Future generations may care for it; others may concrete it over. Who knows what will become of it? Whatever its future, it is your job to care for it now.

The myth of the 'maintenance-free' garden has been perpetrated by television presenters and gardening magazine editors, but no such thing exists! The world does not work that way; it is always changing, evolving and decaying. Your role as caretaker of a garden is to work to enhance and maintain it while enjoying its beauty along the way.

The first and easiest maintenance task is the removal of all dead matter. Dead growth in the plants, dropped leaves and wind-blown debris should regularly be cleared away.

PRUNING TREES AND SHRUBS

A healthy garden grows constantly and pruning will need to be done. It should always be considered as a creative opportunity to bring out a particular tree's 'tree-ness', or to improve a plant's form and beauty. Dead material, or material that has served its function, is removed to enhance the character of the plant and concentrate the viewer's attention (see below for more on pruning). However, pruning can also include grass cutting, re-shaping of herbaceous plants and the clipping or re-shaping of hedges.

Pruning in a Japanese garden has a dual purpose. General pruning is carried out to maintain the health and vigour of the tree, as in any garden, but in a Japanese garden it is also used to create a tree with added interest. If properly done, this type of pruning

Decaying maple leaves, the closing year.

improves the design lines, suggests the passage of time and gives the tree great character.

In nature, trees grow in a certain way and an observation of this helps the Japanese gardener to do 'creative' pruning. As a branch on a young tree grows, it stretches upwards for light. When the branch ages and produces lots of twigs and leaves, gravity counteracts this juvenile surge, and the branch starts to be pulled down by its own weight. Its lower sub-branches, now shaded from the sunlight, start to wither and are eventually shed. During this process, other branches in more favourable positions become dominant. The repetition of this process over many years produces the aged character that is associated with mature trees. When pruning for the garden, it is possible to mimic this natural process and shorten the time that nature takes to achieve the same results. This kind of pruning not only benefits deciduous trees but is essential when pruning pines and many other evergreens.

In Japan, pruning is considered a much more highly skilled task than it is in the West, where it is often carried out by untrained workers. A 'tree surgeon' can cause a significant amount of damage with injudicious use of a chainsaw, and this is evident in many places in the European countryside.

The most common mistake is to let the branch grow too long and then try to rectify matters by cutting straight through the large limb. This produces a huge mass of new buds at the point of the cut, and all these buds will grow for a few years, fattening the branch at that point. Natural selection then takes over and one or two of these sub-branches will become

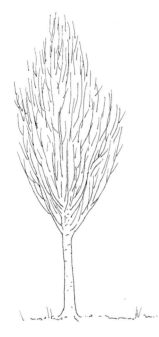

Character in trees young and old – as a tree ages, the passage of its life is reflected in its appearance. In young trees, all the energy is upwards.

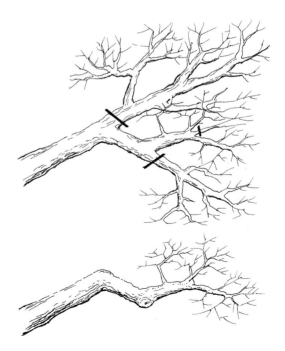

Pruning cuts to develop character in deciduous trees.

dominant and form the new extension of the main branch. By then, the damage is done and the tree is left with a branch that has a swelling where it was cut, a huge scar, no taper in the branch, and sub-branches that grow off at peculiar angles. In short, the result will be a tree that has lost it natural taper and looks deformed rather than aged.

There are two secrets when pruning:

● do not leave it until too drastic measures are needed; and
● always preserve the sap flow-line.

The energy of the branch is always concentrated at its outer ends, as this is where the leaves are and where the new growth takes place. The leaves are the lungs of the tree and are essential to its health. By always cutting to a healthy side-branch, this 'living line' is preserved and the tree is not over-stressed. If all the major branches are cut at the same time, the sap has nowhere to go, and this produces a condition similar to high blood pressure. This problem can be rectified and the stress reduced by cutting through some of the tree's roots to retain the balance between branch and root. However, this should be unnecessary if pruning is done in the right way in the first place.

Different species of tree need different pruning techniques. Pines naturally produce a whorl of branches from one point each year. Only two of these branches – a new leader and one side-shoot – should be retained. The remainder should be removed. If this is not done, a large swelling will appear from the point where the shoots sprouted. This pruning process is done naturally in nature but needs to be done manually in the garden if the tree is to retain its proper taper.

If left to grow unchecked, a pine will produce long, thin, gangly branches, with a little bit of foliage at the ends. If a cut is made through a pine branch, behind where the green needles are growing, it will not regenerate. It will not bud back and produce new growth, as a deciduous tree will. The branch will simply die. With pines, this pruning back to a living side-branch is essential.

Every year, pines also naturally de-needle, shedding their two-year-old needle growth as part of their

ageing process. In Japan, de-needling also takes place as part of the annual pruning and maintenance procedure, when needles from the previous year are manually removed by pulling. This has the effect of allowing light and air to circulate freely and helps the tree to remain healthy. It also stimulates back-budding in the tree, which, in turn, allows correct pruning, as it will be possible to cut further back along the branch to a selection of side-shoots. This constant needle pulling and pruning quickly produces a tree with elegant floating 'cloud-like' foliage, and will assist in developing line and character in the design.

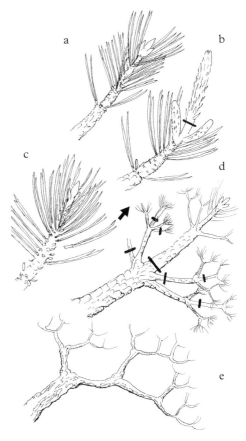

The pruning of a pine tree:
'a' – a shoot of pine showing,
1. this year's growth and the new bud, 2. last year's needles, and 3. needles left from the previous year;
'b' – pruning new growth in spring back to two shoots;
'c' – needle pulling in winter of last year's old needles;
'd' – pruning unwanted growth in pines to develop character;
'e' – the branch after pruning.

Opposite: *Styled pine, Jovuviji Temple.*

Devotional detailed work of this kind is unknown in the West, but in Japan, all the pines of the temples and famous gardens are treated in this way. The pruning of one pine may take two men three or four days to complete, and even very large trees are pruned in this manner. The work is ideally undertaken during the winter months before the new buds swell; if it is done later, too much damage would be caused to the newly developing foliage.

Deciduous trees also need occasional pruning to neaten their appearance. If the tree is young, it will tend always to make new growth at its top and at its branch ends. Any inner growth will gradually lose vigour and die off. Through the removal of the new growth, in early summer, energy is pushed back into the inner areas and vigour is retained. This has the effect of triggering back-budding and produces more twigging, keeping the tree compact in size. Many small ornamental trees, including some of the maples, have a naturally dwarf habit, and this work is seldom necessary.

As with pines, where possible, branching should be pruned back to two shoots – a new leader and one side-shoot. If a branch becomes too long or too vigorous, cutting back to a side-shoot will control the energy while preserving the taper in the branch. This will also allow character to be creatively pruned into the tree.

Existing trees in the garden can be tidied up by cutting back over-long branches to a side-shoot and by removing any branches that cross each other or rub against each other. Pruning is best done in early September, when the trees are making wood rather than leaves. The pruning cuts will then have time to start healing themselves before the winter sets in. Large cuts are best protected with a wound sealant, which retains a flexible skin and contains a fungicide.

WEEDING

Plants that were not originally planned for the garden, usually referred to as 'weeds', will soon start to grow. In some places, they may not be wanted. If they cannot be fitted into the garden's new evolution, they should be removed before they become a problem. If you have used a weed-suppressant membrane, weeding should not be a major preoccupation. The application of a mulch can also be effective for weed control.

FEEDING

As plants grow, nutrients are taken out of the soil, and health and vigour will be lost if the plant cannot find a continuing supply of food. All the plants must be fed periodically if they are to maintain their vigour. In the natural world, the plant would simply die and its place would be taken by another, more vigorous plant. In order to suit the needs of the garden's design, the plant's life must be extended to its ultimate maturity. Only when it has reached its full maturity, or it no longer fits the design, should it be removed.

The number of microbes in any soil will vary depending upon the soil's health and composition. These microbes will only break down organic fertilizer to release nutrients when both plant and soil health are at their optimum level. These nutrients are then absorbed at a rate that is correct for the needs of the plant. Organic fertilizers appear to be absorbed more efficiently than chemical fertilizers. However, chemical fertilizers are fast acting, and can be of great use where the plant needs an immediate boost to its vigour. There is a possibility that chemicals burn the plant's delicate root hairs, but there is definitely a difference in the results when compared with organic fertilizers.

Having tried both organic and chemical fertilizers over many years, I am a devotee of the organic method. It may be less aromatic, but ultimately it seems to work better, and to be safer for the plants. Gardeners in Japan make holes around the base of a plant and drop into them pellets made from organic material. This process is repeated every two to three years. Any of the liquid organic fertilizers on the market can be used, if they are mixed as recommended by the supplier. As an alternative, try making your own pellets from a Japanese recipe that is often used by Bonsai growers. Mix together 70 per cent rapeseed meal, 20 per cent fishmeal and 10 per cent bonemeal, with just enough water so that the mixture can be rolled into balls of about 5cm in diameter. A little straw ash or wood ash (about 10 per cent) can be added to the mixture for plants for which too much acidity is not favourable.

ROOT PRUNING

Winter garden, Kanazawa.

Another maintenance method of restoring vigour involves periodically cutting some of the roots of trees and shrubs so that new soil can be introduced around the plants. This encourages new fine feeder roots to develop and rejuvenate the plant. The root work is usually done just before the plant starts growth in spring, and is often accompanied by the 'creative' pruning of the top of the shrub or tree (see pages 128–132 for information on pruning trees). Over the winter, food has been stored in the plant and in spring it becomes available to produce a new surge of growth. This new growth is then directed towards the production of new roots and the stimulation of those weaker shoots that have been left after the 'creative' pruning.

All the roots are not cut at the same time – the work is spread over several years. This technique is not used on young trees, but only on mature plants that are showing signs of lack of vigour. The trees are not over-stressed as a balance is maintained between branch and root.

PONDS

If the water in the pond is to stay clear and healthy, it will need regular attention throughout the year. Evaporation will mean that the pondwater needs to be topped up on a regular basis throughout the summer; despite this topping-up process, however, the water will still become stale, especially if fish are present. To maintain the health of the pond, half of the water should be changed each spring and autumn. This can easily be achieved by diverting the water from the pump through a hose to a sump area, emptying the pond on one side while filling it from a hosepipe on the other side. Depending on the size of the pond, half the water can be changed in this way in a few hours, with very little disturbance to fish or plants.

A rapid fall in the water level in the pond would indicate a problem somewhere in the system. If the pond has a pump, the pump should be switched off immediately. If the pond's water loss persists, the problem is probably within the pond itself. If the problem stops, there may be a problem in one of the watercourses or waterfalls. If the pump is off, and there is no apparent loss from the whole system, the problem may be one that only persists while the pump is running. It might simply be a question of overflow, splashing or interference from plant growth. If there is no loss from the pond, but there is loss from the system, you should, if possible, isolate each section of the watercourse to locate the leak.

If the leak is within the pond, the level at which the problem has occurred will be evident from the level of the pondwater. Punctures and cracks are never particularly easy to mend and temporary homes may have to be found for fish and plants while the problem is being tackled. However, modern adhesives are becoming more and more effective and, whereas it was once almost impossible to get a really effective watertight seal on repairs, kits are now available to make the repair of smaller leaks a relatively simple task.

Green water, caused by the growth of single-cell free-swimming algae, is a problem that affects most ponds at some time or other. Each individual cell is microscopic but the algae, encouraged by sunlight, can appear in such vast numbers as to make the water in the pond resemble pea soup. Do not be tempted to change the water, as this will only delay the problem, not cure it. Newly filled ponds are rich in mineral salts on which the algae thrive, and the problem will return almost immediately. Although green water looks unsightly, and prevents observation of both fish and plants, it is not normally harmful. Fish much prefer green water to the harsh additives that are present in tapwater. An even balance is usually found between plant life and nutrients after a few weeks and the water will clear. However, if the problem persists, a range of pond-water treatments are available from most pet shops and garden centres. These include remedies to control algae, to de-chlorinate and condition water, and to treat and prevent all manner of fish ailments.

The most effective and ecologically friendly treatment for green water is a natural one – barley straw placed in the pond. This can now be bought neatly packaged in black mesh so that it is not visible under the water. It takes a couple of weeks for the microbes from the decomposing straw to become effective, but it clears algae, keeps the pondwater crystal clear for a whole season without replacement, and is completely harmless to fish.

Blanket weed *Spirogyra* can become a problem, even in clear water. If left unchecked, it can choke water plants and leave little room for fish to swim. Blanket weed is still algae but, instead of being free-swimming, it is in filamentous threads. Manual control is possible. A rough stick twisted among the threads can draw the weed from all over the pond, and a rake can be used with care to comb the threads out of the oxygenating plants. Once it has been collected, remove the blanket weed from the pond as it starts to decompose quickly and will reduce the oxygen level in the water. Removal of blanket weed can be a tiring activity, but it is often interesting because of the wildlife that can be brought out with the threads. Leave the pile of blanket weed by the side of the pond for a short while to give time for the more mobile water creatures to return to the pond.

Where maintenance of plant growth in the pond is concerned, the problem is usually one of too much growth rather than too little. The small bunches of oxygenating plants that were put in when the pond was created will have made masses of growth and will have served their purpose. Their natural function from the autumn onwards, as the water cools, is to die back and sink to the bottom of the pond, where they will decay. Gasses from decomposing plant matter gather under any ice that may form in the winter and will be toxic to fish and other life in the pond. To avoid the problem, cut back any long growth and remove any excess weed in September. Water-lily leaves and stems should be removed before the first frosts, as they decompose very quickly.

Where marginal plants are concerned, it is usually better to cut back the top growth when it has started to die back. This will help to keep the plant stable in the winter winds and keep decaying matter from the pond. Plants that have put on excessive growth during the summer can be removed, have their roots and foliage trimmed back, and can be put back in the pond again. However, if the plant is very delicate, it may be better to remove it to a bucket in a cold greenhouse.

If fallen leaves have been allowed to accumulate in the water, it may become black and foul. This may necessitate a complete clear-out of the pond, and some preventive measure to ensure that the problem does not reoccur. Covering the pond in the autumn with fine black plastic netting – black being less obtrusive than green – will keep most leaves out.

A complete clear-out of the pond should not really be necessary unless there has been a problem with contamination from pesticides, herbicides or excessive decaying matter. After cleaning, the organic balance of the pond will have to be re-established.

During the winter months, it is important to keep part of the surface area clear of ice. A build-up of gasses under the ice will be severely detrimental to any fish or wildlife that might be in the pond. A small ball floating on the water will help to keep an area clear when the weather is not too harsh, but the ice may become really thick during prolonged cold spells. In this case, you may need to melt the ice using a metal container holding very hot water. Applying this repeatedly to the same spot will quite quickly breach even the thickest covering of ice. Small electrically powered water heaters, specifically designed for this purpose, are available and could be useful if there is a power supply near by.

The main thing to remember is that the ice should never be broken by striking with a hammer or any other instrument. Doing this may both damage the pond structure and kill the fish.

GENERAL MAINTENANCE

Although the timber used in any garden structures, bridges or decking will have been pressure-treated with preservatives, it will be necessary from time to time to apply further preservatives to stop the wood from decaying. Check for splits, cracks and rusting of screws or bolts on an annual basis, and replace any badly damaged or decaying parts. Remove any fungal growth with a stiff brush before applying preservatives, and if you are working near plants, make sure that the preservative you use is not detrimental to their growth.

Garden artefacts such as lanterns, bowls or statuary do not generally require any maintenance; in fact, weathering and moss growth often improves their appearance. However, it may be necessary to give some of them an annual washing down to remove green algae. Also, the effect you planned from your artefacts can sometimes be lost in excessive plant growth, so a general tidying up of the whole area surrounding them may be necessary.

For general safety, before the winter sets in, ensure that all electrical connections to garden lights, pumps, and so on, are in good condition, sound and totally weatherproof.

CHAPTER 9

Final Thoughts

While following this path through the Japanese garden we have looked at its history, development, design, construction and maintenance. This book is just a starting point. The path has not come to an end. This path has no end; it is only a way. There is still much more to be found on this journey.

We have deliberately not provided detailed plans of gardens to be followed slavishly; this would crush the spirit of the garden. Study our photographs and drawings for ideas, choose a few elements that fulfil your inner need, and put them together in a way that pleases your eye.

Take time to sit quietly with your garden and a universe will unfold before you. There will be joy as plants grow, tragedies as favourite plants die for no apparent reason, and confusion when your design suddenly seems lost in rampant growth. Such is the way of life and the way of the world, of which your garden is but a part. Never forget that all can be redeemed in a new and different way, a new beginning, ever growing, ever changing.

From the plum tree blossom
Does the fragrance float upwards?
There is a halo around the moon.

Taniguchi Buson (1715–83)

Opposite: *Foliage clouds drift over an ancient island.*

Glossary

Amancha

A sweet tea drunk on Buddha's birthday.

Cha-no-yu

Literally 'hot water of tea' or the 'Way of Tea', another name for the Tea Ceremony, but implying a deeper understanding. Literally, living life with respect for all things.

Chirianu

The small dust or rubbish pit found in the ground in the tea garden. Mostly symbolic of cleanliness and order rather than practical.

Chozubachi

'Hand water basin', often found as part of the tsukubai arrangement; usually made of stone.

Chumon

'Middle gate'. The gate that divides the outer section of the tea garden from the more secluded inner area, which contains the teahouse. Passing through is the reminder to prepare one's inner state for the Tea Ceremony.

Eboshi

A hat worn in the Heian era.

Feng Shui (Chinese)

In Japanese Fusui, translating as 'wind-water'. The system of geomancy inherited from the Chinese that explains the energy patterns that lie within all things.

Gyo

Semi-formal style.

Hagi Tsubo

Courtyard planted with Japanese bush clover.

Hanami

'Flower viewing', usually of Ume or cherry blossom in the spring. Large parties, often workers on their lunch break, gather under the flowering trees.

Ikebana

The ancient Japanese art of arranging flowers.

Ikekomigata

Lanterns that have their pedestals buried in the ground.

Ikedori

'To capture alive' – the term for the techniques used to bring the surrounding landscape into the design of the garden.

Kaiyushiki

The 'stroll garden', developed during the Edo period. Usually, it is quite large, with many features or sights to see.

Kami

The animistic spirits that inhabit special places such as unusual rock formations or ancient ponds. Revered in the Shinto religion.

Karesansui

Literally 'withered mountain water', a term used for the dry stone gardens developed in the Muromachi period for many Zen temples

Kobushi

Translates as 'fist', and is applied to the shape of magnolia flowers.

Koshikake

The roofed waiting bench found in the tea garden where participants sit quietly and prepare for the Tea Ceremony.

Li Chi (Chinese)

The 'Fungus of Immortality' found in many Chinese myths.

Okidoro

Small lanterns that are easily movable.

Roji

Literally 'dewy path' – the name given by the tea masters to the garden that leads to the teahouse and the Tea Ceremony.

Sanzon

A grouping of three stones originally meant to represent a Buddhist Trinity of enlightened beings.

Sasa Tsubo

Courtyard planted with the low-growing bamboo Kumasasa.

Shakkei

The term now used for ikedori, or 'borrowed scenery', the use of distant views as part of a garden's design.

Shin

Formal style.

Shishi odoshi

'Deer scarer' – a device activated by trickling water used to scare deer or birds and prevent damage to the garden.

Shoji

The paper-covered screens that make up the walls of traditional Japanese houses.

So

Informal or rustic style.

Suikinkutso

The echo chamber constructed below a water basin to amplify the sound of dripping water.

Sukiya

A style of architecture inspired by the austerity of teahouse construction.

Tachigata

Lanterns that sit upon their own bases as opposed to having their pedestals buried in the ground.

Tokonoma

The alcove found in the teahouse, and many traditional style buildings, to present a display usually ikebana that reflects the season.

Tsukubai

The arrangement of a water basin (chozubachi) and four stones (yakuishi). Used for ritual purification in the tea garden.

Tsuboniwa

The name for the courtyard garden designed to bring light and freshness into traditional Japanese houses in the Edo period.

Wabi

A difficult-to-define Japanese word suggesting the subdued taste associated with the Tea Ceremony.

Yakuishi

The four stones that surround the water basin in the tsukubai arrangement. A flat front stone stands on a side stone, on which to place a hand-held lantern. A stone on the other side holds a basin of hot water, and a back stone balances the arrangement and makes an uneven number of items.

Yatsubashi

A bridge made from eight wooden planks set at angles to one another, often used in swampy areas.

Yamadoro

Stone lanterns made from beautiful pieces of un-worked stone put together in the form of a lantern. Used in rustic-style situations.

Yamogi Tsubo

A courtyard planted with Artemisia.

Yukimigata

Literally, 'snow-viewing lantern', a lantern designed with a wide top, to collect snow. Often multi-legged and placed near water.

Bibliography

Billington, Jill, *Architectural Foliage*
(Ward Lock, 1991)

Brickell, Christopher (Ed.), *A-Z Encyclopaedia of Garden Plants* (Royal Horticultural Society/Dorling Kindersley, 1996)

Cave, Philip, *Creating Japanese Gardens*
(Aurum Press, 1993)

Hibi, Sadao, *Japan's Best-Loved Gardens*
(Graphic Sha, 1993)

Itoh, Teiji, *Space and Illusion in the Japanese Garden*
(John Weatherhill, 1983)

Japanese Garden Research Association, *Create Your Own Japanese Garden* (Crespi Edition, 1995)

Katsuhiko, Mizuno, *The Gardens of Kyoto*
(Kyoto Shoin, 1987)

Katsuhiko, Mizuno, *Masterpieces of Japanese Gardens*
(Kyoto Shoin, 1992)

Keane, Mac P., *Japanese Garden Design*
(Tuttle, 1996)

Lawson, David, *Secret Teachings in the Art of Japanese Gardens*
(Kodansha International Ltd, 1987)

Lowenstein, Tom, *The Vision of the Buddha*
(Duncan Baird Publishers, 1996)

Ohashi, Haruzo, *The Tea Garden*
(Graphic Sha, 1989)

Ono, Sokyo, Shinto, *The Kami Way* (Tuttle, 1962)

Readers Digest Encyclopaedia of Garden Plants and Flowers (Readers Digest, 1978)

Richards, Betty and Keneko, Anne, *Japanese Plants*
(Shufunotomo, 1988)

Robinson, Peter, *The Water Garden* (Royal Horticultural Society/Conran Octopus, 1994)

Schenk, George, *Moss Gardening*
(Timber Press, Oregon, 1997)

Seike, Kiyoshi, Kudo, Masambu and Engel, David, *A Japanese Touch for Your Garden*
(Kodansha International Ltd, 1986)

Shigemori, Kanto, *The Japanese Courtyard Garden*
(John Weatherhill, 1983)

Yoshikawa, Isao and Osamu, Suzuki, *Bamboo Fences of Japan* (Graphic Sha, 1988)

Yoshikawa, Isao, *Elements of Japanese Gardens*
(Graphic Sha, 1990)

Yoshikawa, Isao, *Japanese Gardening in Small Spaces*
(Premier Book Marketing, 1996)

Yoshikawa, Isao, *The World of Zen Gardens*
(Graphic Sha, 1991)

Index